# THE SCIENCE OF
# SUCCESS

# THE SCIENCE OF
# SUCCESS

## How Market-Based Management Built the World's Largest Private Company

# CHARLES G. KOCH

### CEO, Koch Industries, Inc.

BICENTENNIAL
1807
WILEY
2007
BICENTENNIAL

## John Wiley & Sons, Inc.

Published by John Wiley & Sons, Inc., Hoboken, New Jersey
Published simultaneously in Canada

Wiley Bicentennial Logo: Richard J. Pacifico

Market-Based Management®, MBM®, Koch Industries, Inc.® and Principled Entrepreneurship™ are trademarks of Koch Industries, Inc. Flexitray® is a trademark of Koch-Glitsch, Inc. STAINMASTER® and Lycra® are trademarks of INVISTA North America S.à r.l. Quilted Northern®, Angel Soft®, Brawny®, Dixie®, Dens® and Plytanium® are trademarks of Georgia-Pacific LLC. The preceding trademarks are protected by United States and, where applicable, foreign laws. Any unauthorized use of the preceding trademarks without the express written permission of their owner is a violation of the law.

IBM® is a trademark of International Business Machines Corporation.

For general information on our other products and services or for technical support, please contact our Customer Care Department within the United States at (800) 762-2974, outside the United States at (317) 572-3993 or fax (317) 572-4002.

Wiley also publishes its books in a variety of electronic formats. Some content that appears in print may not be available in electronic books. For more information about Wiley products, visit our web site at www.wiley.com

ISBN-13 978-0-470-13988-2

Printed in the United States of America

10  9  8  7  6  5  4  3  2

# CONTENTS

# PREFACE

*"Keep your obligations and promises. Try, if possible,
to do business with honorable people. All the
contracts and lawyers in Christendom cannot make
a dishonorable man hew to the line."*
—Fred C. Koch[1]

This book introduces Market-Based Management®, the distinctive business and management philosophy that has enabled Koch Industries, Inc. (KII) to become one of the largest and most successful private companies in the world.

Since 1961, the year I came to work for my father, the book value of Koch Industries has increased 2000-fold (assuming reinvestment of dividends). Unusual among large companies, Koch Industries has continued to grow rapidly and profitably as we've become bigger. We are frequently asked how we do it. The answer is simple: MBM®.

We define MBM as a philosophy that enables organizations to succeed long term by applying the principles that allow free societies to prosper. We think and talk about it in terms of five dimensions: vision, virtue and talents, knowledge processes, decision rights and incentives. I wish to note two main points about this list. First, we understand and use these terms somewhat differently than they typically appear in management literature. For example, vision for us is not a one-time statement of goals and aspirations, but a dynamic concept, always evolving based on continual examination of how we can create value for our customers and for society. Because of this, our businesses' visions must—and do—change.

Second, while we describe MBM in terms of five dimensions, the approach is more than simply a sum of the parts. When these dimensions and their underlying concepts are understood holistically and applied in an integrated, mutually reinforcing manner, the effect is continuously transformative. Just as living things are more than a collection of molecules, organizations that combine all these factors become something beyond an ordinary collection of people, activities and assets.

Our MBM framework was not always so well-defined. In fact, it took many years for our everyday practices and mental models to come together in the way they are framed in this book. Our current MBM framework was first articulated in the early 1990s, but it evolved from much older concepts and models.

Some key aspects of MBM, such as the emphasis on values and entrepreneurship, came from my father, who co-founded the company that would become Koch Industries. He exemplified much of what is centrally important to us: the value of hard work, integrity, humility and a lifelong dedication to learning.

The most important source was my own reading and study. Shortly after joining Rock Island Oil (the predecessor of Koch Industries), I developed two strong passions. The first was to help build a great company. The second was to identify and understand the principles that lead to prosperity and societal progress. After studying history, economics, philosophy, science, psychology and other disciplines, I concluded that the two passions were strongly, indeed intimately, related.

Of the many great books I read, two really helped start me on my intellectual journey: F. A. Harper's *Why Wages Rise* and Ludwig von Mises' *Human Action*. Harper's book clearly identifies the causes of real, sustainable wage increases and distinguishes them from illusory increases. He explains that real wages are determined by the marginal productivity of labor. In *Human Action*, Mises argues that a market economy based on private property and the rule of law promotes civility, peace and prosperity.

As an engineer, I understood the natural world operated according to fixed laws. Through my studies, I came to realize that there were, likewise, laws that govern human well-being. I learned that prosperity is only possible in a system where property rights are clearly and properly defined and protected, people are free to speak, exchange and contract, and prices are free to guide beneficial action. Allowing people the freedom to pursue their own interests, within beneficial rules of just conduct, is the best and only sustainable way to promote societal progress.

It seemed to me that these laws are fundamental not only to the well-being of societies, but also to the miniature societies of organizations. Indeed, that is what we found when we began to apply the laws systematically at Koch Industries.

The third source of MBM is the experience gained and lessons learned as we've tried new approaches, innovated, stumbled, succeeded and continued to grow and change. Our philosophy and practice have evolved with us, and we expect them to continue to do so in the future.

———————

This book devotes a chapter to each dimension of MBM. In writing it, I've had two audiences in mind. First is the broad audience of present and future employees of Koch Industries. The book is intended to explain our philosophy and why we think and act as we do. I hope it will help our employees maximize their contributions and realize their full potential. Each employee, moreover, can help us experiment and improve our understanding of how to get results through MBM.

The second audience I have in mind is broader and consists of business readers. MBM is not just another list of qualities of a successful company so common in today's management literature. It is a way for business to create a harmony of interest with society. For business to survive and prosper, it must create real long-term value in society through principled behavior.

MBM works because it is grounded in consistent, valid theory that is fully integrated and applied across every aspect of the organization. It certainly has worked well for Koch Industries, and there's no reason why it cannot also work well for other organizations. I believe this book will help any principled individual or organization striving to create real, long-term value.

I am convinced the combination of our market-based philosophy and how we practice it has been the primary source of our success. But past performance does not guarantee future success. To continue to achieve superior results, we must continually improve our understanding and application of MBM. Just as the market economy is a journey of experimental discovery toward an unknown future of increasing societal prosperity, so MBM is a never-ending process of learning and improvement. Like the North Star, it is not a goal in itself, but a guide—in this instance toward greater and greater value creation. To all readers of this book who endeavor to understand and apply these principles, I wish you every success on this journey.

*Charles G. Koch*
Wichita, Kansas
January 2007

# ACKNOWLEDGMENTS

I thank all those associates who, over the last 40-some years, have helped us begin to understand how to apply Market-Based Management® to achieve results. In particular, Rich Fink and Steve Daley provided invaluable advice and assistance in creating this book. I also thank Rod Learned, who greatly improved the book by his edits. Any errors or oversights, however, are solely mine.

Additionally, I thank my brother David and the Marshall family, the best business partners anyone could wish for. Most of all, I thank my wife of 34 years, Liz. Her steadfast love, support and guidance changed my life. Without these three partnerships, none of this would have been possible.

*Charles G. Koch*
January 2007

*"Don't take counsel of your fears."*

Fred C. Koch[1]

# CHAPTER 1

# EVOLUTION OF A BUSINESS

*"He that would know what shall be,*
*must consider what hath been."*

—H. G. Bohn[2]

*"In truth, there is no such thing as a growth industry.*
*There are only companies organized and operated to create*
*and capitalize on growth opportunities. Industries*
*that assume themselves to be riding some automatic*
*growth escalator invariably descend into stagnation."*

—Theodore Levitt[3]

An understanding of MBM® and how it served to guide and build Koch Industries is helped by a brief review of the company's evolution.

A good starting place is my grandfather, Harry Koch, who was trained as a printer's apprentice. He emigrated from the Netherlands in 1888 and three years later settled in Quanah, Texas, where he bought a struggling weekly newspaper and print shop. That newspaper, the *Tribune-Chief*, is still published today.

Quanah was in a very poor area, so many of Harry's customers paid, in part, with barter. My father, Fred C. Koch, born in 1900, saw little future in Quanah or the printing business. He left to study engineering at Rice, where he was elected president of his sophomore class. He transferred to MIT upon learning it had created the first-ever chemical engineering program. He became captain of the boxing team at MIT, where he graduated in 1922. Following graduation, my father was employed as a chemical engineer by three different companies.

In 1925, he was invited by an MIT classmate to become a partner in an engineering firm in Wichita, Kansas. Two years after joining that firm, which was renamed the Winkler-Koch Engineering Company, my father developed an improved thermal cracking process for converting heavy oil into gasoline. His development was less expensive and increased yields with less downtime.

Winkler-Koch's success in selling this process to independent refiners immediately caught the attention of the major oil companies. To control the technology, most of the majors had pooled their cracking patents into what was known as the Patent Club, coordinated by the Universal Oil Products Company (UOP). Then, as now, UOP was the leading refinery process development company. The difference was, back then, UOP was owned by the majors.

Unlike my father's development, which was royalty-free, the Patent Club charged a high royalty. In 1929, the Patent Club—worried about the increased competitiveness of the independents—sued Winkler-Koch and all its customers, alleging patent infringement. This crippled Winkler-Koch's business in the U.S. It survived by building plants abroad, especially in the Soviet Union where it built 15 cracking units. As a result, Winkler-Koch enjoyed its first real financial success during the early years of the Great Depression.

Fred found the Soviet Union to be "a land of hunger, misery and terror." Virtually all the Soviet engineers he worked with were purged by Stalin, who exterminated tens of millions of his own people. This experience, combined with what his Communist associates told him of their methods and plans for world revolution, caused my father to become a staunch anti-Communist.

Throughout 23 years of lawsuits with the Patent Club, Winkler-Koch only lost one, and even that verdict was overturned when it was discovered the judge had been bribed. The resulting scandal was so great that the majors "donated" UOP to the American Chemical Society. Winkler-Koch countersued, settling in 1952 for $1.5 million. Although that was a sizeable sum, it prompted my father to advise me to "never sue; the lawyers get a third, the government gets a third and you get your business destroyed." I've tried to follow his advice and have filed very few lawsuits. Unfortunately, he forgot to tell me how to keep from being sued.

In 1940, Fred accepted an offer to join a new company being formed to build a 10,000-barrel-per-day refinery near East St. Louis. This company, the Wood River Oil & Refining Co., Inc., was the predecessor of Koch Industries. My father, one of five initial stockholders, was recruited to design and operate the plant. He bought a 23 percent interest in the company for $230,000.

Wood River got off to a rough start, hampered by a 90 percent "excess profits" tax during World War II and a conflict that arose among the original stockholders. In 1944, two of those stockholders sold their shares back to the company. In 1946, Wood River acquired an 8,000-barrel-per-day refinery and a 10,000-barrel-per-day crude oil gathering system near Duncan, Oklahoma, for $400,000 and a 10 percent interest in Wood River. (Gathering systems transport crude oil from the wellhead to a major pipeline.) These assets were placed in a new, wholly-owned subsidiary, Rock Island Oil & Refining Co., Inc. This refinery was shut down in 1949, but the gathering system became the foundation for Wood River's largest business.

In 1950, the Wood River refinery was sold and the remaining original stockholders sold their interests back to the company. My father retained the Wood River name and used most of the residual proceeds to buy ranches in Montana and Texas. These became his primary focus, along with the development of fractionation devices (used to separate liquids by boiling point differences). Other ventures included fiberglass pipe, camping trailers and cooling towers for homes. He even retrofitted a small fleet of bombers into corporate aircraft, but without success.

## THE KASKADE TRAY

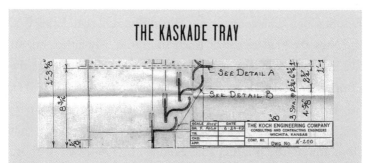

Fred C. Koch's innovative design for the Kaskade fractionation tray was introduced by Koch Engineering in 1949. It promised 50 percent more capacity with 25 percent better efficiency, but only at a very narrow throughput range. If its load increased or decreased even slightly, efficiency declined significantly.

Koch gave up on the Kaskade design after a customer accidentally installed the tray upside down and discovered it worked better that way.

As if these business challenges were not enough, my father also had to deal with a houseful of rambunctious boys. I was born in 1935, the second of four. By instilling a work ethic in me at an early age, my father did me a big favor, although it didn't seem like a favor back then. By the time I was eight, he made sure work occupied most of my spare time.

I was not an exemplary student in my early years, but I improved and was accepted at MIT, where I graduated with a bachelor's and two master's degrees in engineering. Following graduation, I stayed in Boston and went to work for Arthur D. Little, Inc. (ADL), a leading consulting firm.

After about two years at ADL my father began pressuring me to return to Wichita and join the family firm. Since I was learning a lot and enjoyed what I was doing, I turned him down. Finally, he made me an offer I couldn't refuse. He said his health was poor, and if I didn't come back to run the company, he would sell it.

By 1961, the company's name had been changed to Rock Island Oil & Refining Co., Inc. Its businesses, besides ranching, were a crude oil gathering system in southern Oklahoma and a 35 percent interest in the Great Northern Oil Company (GNOC). The interest in GNOC, which owned what was then a 35,000-barrel-per-day refinery near St. Paul, Minnesota, had been acquired in 1959 from Sinclair Oil. (Over the years, we have continually expanded this refinery and it will soon be nearly ten times that capacity.) Great Northern's other major stockholders were Pure Oil and GNOC's co-founder, J. Howard Marshall II.

My father stressed the importance of humility as well as hard work. When I arrived in Wichita, his first words to me were: "I hope your first deal is a loser, otherwise you will think you're a lot smarter than you are." He had nothing to worry about—I got us in plenty of losers.

My first assignment was to clean up the mess Koch Engineering faced in Europe, caused by having multiple contractors manufacture our fractionation trays in various countries. At that time, the company, which was owned separately from Rock Island by my three brothers and me, had only one plant, in Wichita, making one product—the Flexitray®—a fractionation device. Over the next several years, I spent a great deal of time in Europe setting up our own engineering and manufacturing site outside of Bergamo, Italy. Surprisingly, my father gave me almost complete freedom in the management of Koch Engineering. He told me I could do anything I wanted with it, short of selling it.

Koch Engineering was an indirect offshoot of Winkler-Koch, which never recovered from its decades-long lawsuits with the Patent Club. By 1944, my father and Lewis Winkler no longer shared the same vision for their company, so their partnership was dissolved. My father carried on the engineering business by forming Koch Engineering in 1945. It was two-thirds owned by my brothers and me, and one-third by Harry Litwin, its president. In 1954, Harry Litwin agreed to take the engineering business and form his own company while Koch Engineering retained the Flexitray business.

By the time I moved to Wichita, Koch Engineering had deteriorated to less than $2 million in sales and was barely breaking even. My response, besides setting up our own manufacturing in Europe, was to improve the marketing of Flexitrays and get us into related product lines, such as tower packing, mist eliminators and pollution control equipment. This approach was quite successful. I was named president of Koch Engineering in 1963, and by 1965 sales had more than doubled with a good return.

At this point I began to immerse myself, not only in building the company, but in understanding the principles that lead to prosperity and societal progress. I spent virtually all my spare time studying history and the humane sciences. As I learned concepts that seemed relevant to business, I started to apply them.

As a vice president of Rock Island, I also began working to build that company's largest business—crude oil gathering. My ally in this effort was Sterling Varner, who later became president and COO of KII. We aggressively bought trucks and trucking companies, as well as built and bought pipelines.

My father was supportive of these activities, but, given his poor health, wanted the company to retain sufficient liquidity to pay his estate taxes. As he was preparing to leave for an overseas trip, Sterling and I requested approval to buy two crude oil trucking companies in North Dakota. He gave us approval to buy one, but as soon as he left the country we bought them both. When I informed him of this, my father was initially furious, but eventually forgave us since both acquisitions ended up being highly profitable.

As the growth of our crude oil gathering business accelerated, my father's fragile health deteriorated. In 1966 he made me president of Rock Island so that, as he put it, if something happened to him I would be in charge. In May of 1967 he had a severe heart attack and another, in November, which was fatal. We renamed Rock Island in his honor, and our company has been known as Koch Industries ever since. I was blessed to work with my father for six years until his death. He had a great influence on me and the company. He was a John Wayne-type figure, charismatic and forceful, with great integrity and humility and an insatiable thirst for knowledge. At age 32, I succeeded him as chairman and CEO.

In the years that followed, Sterling and I continued to build our crude oil gathering business. Under Sterling's leadership, it grew to become the largest crude purchaser and gatherer in the U.S. and Canada, growing in volume from 60,000 barrels per day in 1960 to more than 1 million barrels per day in 1990.

This success started with our vision, which was to provide the quickest and best service and to develop the best relations with all producers and explorers. We had a truck at a well site to move the oil as soon as the well began producing. We also developed the capability to build pipelines and to operate pipelines and trucks more economically than our competitors.

We were willing to build a pipeline into a new field without a commitment from the producers as soon as there was any indication it would be economic. Other pipeline companies typically attempted to reduce their risk by requiring a commitment, a reserve study and a fixed tariff. This delayed building the pipeline and created a burden for the producers. Our willingness to move quickly, absorb more risk and give better service enabled us to become the leading crude oil gathering company.

As our crude oil volume grew, at times it was hard to sell all the oil, so we began to build a crude oil trading capability. This was the origin of KII's trading businesses. We also began seeking other commodities for which our capabilities could create superior value.

In 1970, under the leadership of Bill Hanna (president and COO of KII from 1987 to 1999) and Bill Caffey (who became an executive vice president of KII and then of Georgia-Pacific), we moved into gas liquids gathering, fractionation and trading, eventually building it into the largest such business in the country. Using the capabilities developed in gas liquids, we then built a natural gas gathering, transportation, processing and trading business.

In turn, the gas business, together with our other relevant capabilities, enabled the creation of a nitrogen fertilizer business. Koch Nitrogen has since become a leading international fertilizer manufacturing, distributing, marketing and trading company.

One of the most significant events in the evolution of the company was our 1969 acquisition of controlling interest in the Great Northern Oil Company. This brought us back to running a refining business for the first time in nearly 20 years. In 1968, I approached Union Oil (which had acquired Pure Oil) about buying their 40 percent interest in GNOC. They responded by offering it at a price considerably above market, which I declined. Union Oil then began trying to sell its interest to independent refining companies, suggesting that prospective buyers could gain control by also acquiring J. Howard Marshall's interest.

To counter this move, I approached J. Howard with the idea of pooling our interests into a holding company, Koch

Financial Corp., which would be owned in proportion to our interests in Great Northern. I promised we would exchange J. Howard's 30 percent interest in Koch Financial for Koch Industries shares, making him a KII shareholder, when it could be done tax-efficiently. J. Howard readily agreed. His cooperation and trust enabled us to buy Union Oil's GNOC shares, and ultimately all the others, at a reasonable price.

This acquisition brought new capabilities to Koch Industries and led to many new opportunities. Thanks in large part to the leadership of Joe Moeller (president and COO of KII from 1999 to 2005, when he became CEO of Georgia-Pacific), we have grown refining 10-fold. We have also used refining as a base to enter chemicals and, more recently, fibers and polymers.

We entered the chemical business by acquiring Sun Oil's Corpus Christi refinery and chemical complex in 1981. That facility has since been expanded more than five-fold. In 1998, KII entered the fibers and polymers business by acquiring half of Hoechst's polyester business, an opportunity that arose because we were a large supplier of their principal raw material. After acquiring the other half in 2001, we went on to acquire DuPont's nylon, spandex and polyester business, INVISTA, in 2004. INVISTA is one of the world's largest integrated fiber producers with some of the most globally recognized fiber brands, such as STAINMASTER® carpet and LYCRA® spandex.

Refining also provided a base to enter the asphalt business as well as the trading and distribution of other commodities, such as petroleum coke and sulfur. We then added other solid commodities—such as pulp and paper, magnetite, coal and cement—to manufacture, distribute or trade. Koch Exploration, unlike most companies in oil and gas exploration, is also guided by a trading vision.

Over the years, we have constantly extended the list of products we trade and added to our trading capabilities. To do this, we've had to build worldwide coverage and physical assets as well as world-class market knowledge and quantitative analysis. Given our breadth of products, KII is one of the largest traders on the New York Mercantile Exchange (see Appendix A).

The quantitative and risk management capabilities we developed for commodity trading helped us build a financial trading business. Our surplus liquidity, combined with the capabilities gained from our 1992 acquisition of Chrysler's municipal leasing business, allowed us to create a separate, diversified financial business.

Thanks to my brother David's leadership, KII has grown its process equipment and engineering business more than 500-fold. David joined Koch Engineering in 1970 as a technical services manager and became president of Koch Engineering in 1979. He has greatly expanded and broadened its product lines and capabilities, transforming them into Koch Chemical Technology Group (KCTG). It is now a leader in a number of process technologies, including mass transfer, combustion, heat transfer and membrane separation.

In 2001 we began building our Business Development Group, improving the capability to explore other industries for opportunities that fit our capabilities. We had previously identified forest products as one of those industries, and in 2004, Business Development facilitated the acquisition of two small forest products businesses. After unsuccessfully pursuing a number of related businesses, we succeeded in acquiring industry leader Georgia-Pacific (GP) in 2005. This $21 billion acquisition is KII's largest to-date. It provides Koch Industries with a significant growth platform in the forest and consumer products industries. Georgia-Pacific is the world's largest tissue supplier, with many leading North American consumer product brands, such as Quilted Northern®, Angel Soft®, Brawny® and Dixie®. GP is also a leader in other segments of the forest products industry, particularly building products and packaging, with prominent brands such as Dens® wallboard and Plytanium® plywood.

KII's growth over the years was made possible by the fact that J. Howard and his son, Pierce, David Koch and I shared a vision of building a large, entrepreneurial company that generated superior returns. In our view, this required running it as a meritocracy, with positions, authorities and compensation—including that of shareholders—set according to proven ability and actual contributions. This vision also required that the company reinvest most of its earnings. Thus, shareholders had to be willing to forgo larger dividends in the short term to enable the growth that would lead to much greater dividends over the long term. Embracing this vision required both trust and a low time preference.

Today, Koch Industries consists of ten major business groups (see Appendix B) plus the Matador Cattle Co. and a ventures group, Koch Genesis. Matador is the tenth-largest cow/calf operation in the U.S. Koch Genesis is focused on acquiring technologies and technology companies that can significantly enhance our existing businesses.

This brief company history may leave the impression that our experience has been one of ever-improving results, with one success after another, each building on the one before. Nothing could be further from the truth. Progress, whether in business, an economy or science, comes through experimentation and failure. Given that a market economy is an experimental discovery process, business failures are inevitable and any attempt to eliminate them only ensures overall failure. The key is to recognize when we are experimenting and limit the bet accordingly.

Koch companies have suffered when we forgot we were experimenting and made bets as if we knew what we were doing. One of the most extreme cases was our overblown petroleum and tanker trading in the early 1970s. When the Arab oil cutback hit in 1973 and 1974, we were caught with positions beyond our capability to handle, leaving us with large losses. That was certainly a great learning experience, but I'm not sure I could stand that much learning again.

Another experiment that got out of control was our attempt to apply our core capabilities model to agriculture. Here, we jumped immediately from theory to full-scale application, neglecting to apply our experimental discovery model. We were going to produce superior steaks to sell at premium prices, revolutionize milling and baking, convert garbage into animal feed (with what we wrongly thought was great technology) and bring about several other breakthroughs in agriculture. Alas, none of this came to pass and we again suffered sizeable losses.

These weren't KII's only business failures (see Appendix C). There have been a number of others. It is worth noting, however, that many of the businesses we have exited were not failures. They were successes, but had simply reached a point in their life cycle where they no longer provided a core capability or served as a platform for growth. As such, they became more valuable to someone else.

Business failures weren't the only obstacles KII faced. We also encountered partner issues and decades-long lawsuits similar to what my father endured. I believe most of our partner problems were driven by a conflict in visions.

KII's lawsuits spilled into the public arena, amplifying the negative effect of increased regulation, politicization and litigation. They stimulated an onslaught of government investigations and media attacks in the 1980s and 1990s. To survive, we decided we must build a world-class public sector capability, which we did, under the leadership of Rich Fink. This was done by applying the five dimensions of MBM in legal, government and community relations, communications and compliance.

Our Public Sector Capability brought about a retooling of almost every aspect of Koch Industries, including employee selection, development and compensation; the businesses we enter and exit; selection of business leaders; information systems; and ongoing, intensive employee education and training. As a corporation, we not only had to be committed to conducting "all affairs lawfully and with integrity," we had to develop systems to ensure that every employee was committed to—and able to fully comply with—this primary Guiding Principle.

Given all the complex, confusing and ever-changing government mandates, it took years and repeated setbacks to build an effective compliance program. We improved, but we weren't where we needed to be. It required a monumental undertaking to integrate compliance into every aspect of the company. Today, KII's compliance program covers 20 compliance areas, from antitrust to environment to safety. It involves selection, deselection, training, systems, self-assessments, audits, legal integration and even exiting certain businesses. Making it truly effective required broadening our view of who should be held responsible.

As we became much more effective in compliance and defending ourselves, our growth rate accelerated again. I believe our ability to maintain that growth rate will be a direct function of the rate at which we improve our ability to apply MBM. Today, we are generating many more innovations and opportunities—both large and small, internally and externally—than ever before. But we do not intend to rest on our laurels. Every day we are striving to better apply MBM to make Koch Industries an even more exciting, fulfilling place to work.

Doing that—better applying MBM—requires a deep understanding of the dimensions of MBM. Even more, it requires ensuring that all dimensions are in harmony and reinforce each other. The remainder of this book addresses these dimensions and how the Science of Human Action was used to develop them.

"*The solution of the economic problem is a voyage of exploration into the unknown, an attempt to discover new ways of doing things better.*"

F.A. Hayek[1]

# CHAPTER 2

# THE SCIENCE OF HUMAN ACTION

*"The man who grasps principles can successfully select his own methods. The man who tries methods, ignoring principles, is sure to have trouble."*

—Ralph Waldo Emerson[2]

*"Regardless of whether you are an entrepreneur or whether you are an employee of a large company, the absolute prerequisite is that you must know your stuff. There is no substitute for this."*

—Fred C. Koch[3]

M arket-Based Management® is a holistic approach to management that integrates theory and practice and prepares organizations to deal successfully with the challenges of growth and change. The theory of MBM® is rooted in the Science of Human Action.

This science is the study of how humans can best achieve their ends through purposeful behavior. It draws on the disciplines of economics, ethics, social philosophy, psychology, sociology, biology, anthropology, management, epistemology and the philosophy of science.

Market-Based Management also draws on the lessons learned from the successes and failures of humans to achieve peace, prosperity and societal progress. Thus, it includes the study of the history of economies, societies, cultures, politics, governments, conflicts, businesses, non-profits, science and technology.

**MBM IS APPLIED THROUGH FIVE DIMENSIONS:**

| | |
|---|---|
| VISION | Determining where and how the organization can create the greatest long-term value |
| VIRTUE AND TALENTS | Helping ensure that people with the right values, skills and capabilities are hired, retained and developed |
| KNOWLEDGE PROCESSES | Creating, acquiring, sharing and applying relevant knowledge, and measuring and tracking profitability |
| DECISION RIGHTS | Ensuring the right people are in the right roles with the right authorities to make decisions and holding them accountable |
| INCENTIVES | Rewarding people according to the value they create for the organization |

Each of these dimensions will be discussed in detail, but the most important thing about them—indeed, the real power of MBM—is the way the dimensions become mutually reinforcing when applied systematically and consistently over time. That certainly has been our experience at Koch Industries.

## MBM AT KOCH INDUSTRIES

Koch Industries is a leading maker of natural resource-based products, including gasoline, chemicals, polymers, fibers, building products, packaging, tissue and process equipment.

We also trade a wide range of products from commodities to financial instruments. We have a strong record of long-term performance and are widely recognized as one of the world's largest and most successful private companies. For 2006, our annual revenues were about $90 billion—up from $70 million in 1960. As shown in Figure 1, an investment of $1,000 in Koch Industries in 1960 would have a book value of $2 million today (assuming reinvestment of dividends)—a return 16 times higher than what a similar investment in the S&P 500 would have achieved.

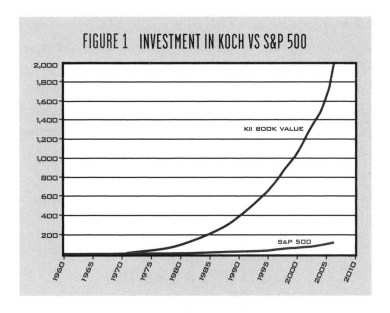

FIGURE 1   INVESTMENT IN KOCH VS S&P 500

It is worth noting that our rapid growth has continued even after becoming a large organization with about 80,000 employees. Such results are uncommon among large companies. In

1917, for example, *Forbes* produced its first list of the 100 largest companies in the United States. Seventy years later, *Forbes* found that only 31 of those companies were still independent and only 18 remained among the 100 largest in the country. Just two outperformed the market average. Despite all their assets and capabilities, the vast majority of the nation's largest companies could not keep pace.

Our approach to management has enabled us to succeed through decades of dramatic change. Energy prices have risen and fallen in repeated cycles, global competition has intensified, the geopolitical map of the world has been redrawn, the volume of regulation and litigation has soared, new technologies have transformed industries and businesses, and the pace of innovation has accelerated.

Koch Industries has grown through these decades because we've learned to embrace change. Change is ever-present in the marketplace. Companies, products and methods are constantly being replaced by more effective alternatives. Economist Joseph Schumpeter famously described this as a process of creative destruction.

## JOSEPH SCHUMPETER
## ON CREATIVE DESTRUCTION

"The...process of industrial mutation...incessantly revolutionizes the economic structure from within, incessantly destroying the old one, incessantly creating a new one. This process of creative destruction is the essential fact of capitalism."

"It is not [price and output] competition which counts, but competition from the new commodity, the new technology, the new source of supply, the new type of organization."[4]

Even successful companies struggle to keep up because, given human nature, we tend to become complacent, self-protective and less innovative as we become successful. It is often more difficult to overcome success than adversity. At Koch Industries, we have countered this tendency, in part, by relentlessly applying our business philosophy. MBM teaches that we must continually drive constructive change in every aspect of our company or we will fail. As a result, we constantly pursue innovations and opportunities through internal and external development and acquisition. Similarly, we shed businesses and assets that are unprofitable or worth more to others. We believe it is essential to drive creative destruction internally, otherwise creative destruction will drive us out of business.

## ORIGINS OF MBM

MBM is based on the principles that cause societies to become prosperous rather than mired in poverty. It views the organization as a miniature society with unique characteristics requiring adaptation of the lessons drawn from society at large. Through this adaptation we have developed our MBM framework and ever-evolving mental models.

## MENTAL MODELS

Mental models are intellectual structures that enable us to simplify and organize the myriad inputs we get from the world around us. They shape and support our thinking, decision making, opinions, values and beliefs. As Ludwig von Mises pointed out: "They are a necessary requirement of any intellectual grasp of historical events."[5] According to Michael Polanyi, they are also vital to scientific progress: "It is by his assimilation of the framework of science that the scientist makes sense of his experience."[6] To be beneficial rather than destructive, our mental models must connect us to reality. Further, they must improve our ability to assimilate new experiences. In the process, they are refined by experience.

Unfortunately, not all mental models reflect reality. People used to believe that the earth was flat and behaved accordingly, even though no one actually found and fell off the edge of the earth. One consequence of this flawed thinking was that many spectacular discoveries were delayed until certain innovators, such as Christopher Columbus, challenged that mental model.

The quality of our mental models determines how well we function in the natural world, and the same is true in the economic world. Thus, Koch Industries invests tremendous time and effort to ensure that our MBM mental models fit reality and are understood and applied throughout our businesses. A business with behavior based on faulty mental models is doomed to extinction. We must constantly remind ourselves that just because we believe or want a thing to be true does not make it so.

As Senator Daniel Patrick Moynihan put it: "Everyone is entitled to his own opinions, but not his own facts."[7]

Good mental models, besides being based on reality, should lead to effective action, which introduces additional requirements. They must be neither overly complicated nor too simple, missing key drivers or secondary consequences. They should be checked whenever we don't get the results we anticipated. As with everything, they must always be challenged and improved. We need to constantly ask ourselves if we, in our own way, are thinking and behaving as if the world were flat.

As indicated, MBM is the Science of Human Action applied in an organization. Systematic study of classics in history, economics, philosophy, psychology and other disciplines reveals certain laws that govern human well-being.

This study leads us to conclude that long-term, widespread prosperity is only possible in free societies. Life for the overwhelming majority of people who haven't been blessed to live in a free society has been, as Hobbes put it, "poor, nasty, brutish and short."[8]

## ECONOMIC FREEDOM AND PROSPERITY

The Index of Economic Freedom takes into account many factors that affect the ability of people in a particular country to choose how they work, produce, consume and invest.

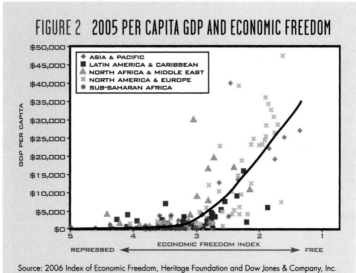

FIGURE 2  2005 PER CAPITA GDP AND ECONOMIC FREEDOM

Source: 2006 Index of Economic Freedom, Heritage Foundation and Dow Jones & Company, Inc.

Economic freedom is strongly correlated with income per capita, as well as other important measures of well-being such as life expectancy, environmental quality, health, education and reduced poverty rates.

The Science of Human Action applies not only at the macro level of societies and nations but also at the micro level of individual organizations. It took me some time to see how understanding the conditions that lead to prosperity could contribute to our efforts to build the company. It became clear because, as I learned introductory economic concepts, such as opportunity cost, subjective value and comparative advantage, I instinctively began to apply them in our company. As I did so, I was surprised to find that, while some of these concepts were taught in economic departments and business schools, they were rarely and inconsistently applied in actual practice.

An example from the late 1960s concerned one such introductory concept that, in spite of being widely taught, was not widely practiced. We were addressing the question of when to sell some inventory. I suggested selling it immediately, but was told the price was below what we had initially paid, so we should wait until it recovered. I pointed out that this shouldn't be the test, because what we paid was now a sunk cost.

## SUNK COST

A sunk cost is an unrecoverable past expenditure. Such costs should seldom be taken into account when determining what to do in the future because, other than possible tax effects, they are irrelevant to what can be recovered.

Instead, I argued our test should be forward-looking and governed by the standard of opportunity cost. We should only hold the inventory if we have strong evidence that the price is likely to rise rather than fall further.

## OPPORTUNITY COST

Opportunity cost is the value of the most valuable alternative that must be forgone to undertake a given act. In decision making, we must look at opportunity cost rather than book or sunk costs. That is, we must look forward rather than backward.

Later, we found even more powerful ways to apply the concept of opportunity cost. To encourage entrepreneurship among our employees, including appropriate risk-taking, we began to consider the profit forgone from an opportunity missed to be equivalent to a book loss resulting from a failed venture.

In another example, I urged our salespeople to understand each customer's subjective values and to tailor the way we dealt with them accordingly.

## SUBJECTIVE VALUE

All economic value derives from people valuing a good, not its cost. Because value is subjective, it is not measurable. Only a person's action, not what he says, gives us an indication of how he values something. This is called demonstrated preference. If someone buys an apple, we know he values the apple more than the price plus the time and effort to make the purchase. Thus, there is no such thing as an even trade. For any exchange to occur, both parties must believe they will gain.

Given the choice, people will satisfy their highest values first. This leads to the concept of diminishing marginal utility. Since people satisfy their highest values first, each subsequent unit of a good will be put to a lower-valued use. This explains why something as abundant as water, while much more valuable than diamonds in total, is much less valued at the margin.

The concept of comparative advantage is another good example. After learning how this principle enhanced prosperity through trade, we applied it to the allocation of roles within a team or business. As we began to hire large numbers of new employees and move existing employees into new roles, we applied this principle by placing employees in roles that best fit their capabilities in relation to both other roles and other employees. This requires a continual reassessment of roles and responsibilities. Otherwise, placement gradually retrogresses by becoming based on absolute rather than comparative advantage, lessening its effectiveness. When replacing someone on a team, the new individual is typically given the same roles as the previous person. Instead, all related roles should be re-optimized.

## COMPARATIVE ADVANTAGE

Nations, organizations or individuals have a comparative advantage for those productive activities in which they create the greatest value relative to the value of the activities forgone. Two entities both gain by trading with each other, even if one is productively superior to the other in all products. The superior producer gains by concentrating on the production of the products for which it has the greatest relative superiority. The disadvantaged producer gains by concentrating on the production for which it is least disadvantaged.

> Just as all nations have comparative advantages that make trade beneficial—even when one country does most things more effectively than another—even the most disadvantaged individuals have comparative advantages.

In the 1960s and 1970s, we were small enough that these market concepts could be infused informally throughout the company's leadership. In every meeting, I would mentor our people by raising relevant questions, such as: "Have we considered the opportunity cost or comparative advantage?" Seeing the power of such basic concepts, I became intrigued by the potential power of more advanced concepts and derivative models. For example, it seemed apparent that in commodity businesses with overcapacity, the price would be set at the cost of the marginal producer. We call this a price-setting mechanism.

## PRICE-SETTING MECHANISM

Price-setting mechanisms are complicated concepts that require an understanding of the meaning of marginal supplier. At the risk of oversimplification, the marginal supplier is the highest-cost producer who reduces production when it is unprofitable. In times of surplus capacity, competition tends to drive the price down to either the incremental or the full cost of the marginal producer (depending on the nature of the industry). This is the price that allows it to break even on either the last unit sold or its entire production.

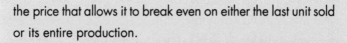

FIGURE 3  PRICE-SETTING MECHANISM

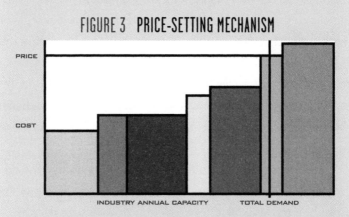

Each bar represents a plant. The height represents each plant's cost and the width its capacity. The lowest-cost plant is shown on the left and the highest-cost on the right. The chart helps predict what the price will be during times of surplus capacity based on our view of future demand.

The chart also indicates the competitive position of each plant. It is a useful tool for competitive and investment analysis and for estimating the effect of changes in demand, cost and capacity on price.

The model shown in Figure 3 helped us improve our ability to predict price movements and to determine the competitive position of each of our facilities. Ultimately, it became a building block of what we call our Decision Making Framework (DMF), which we consider one of our more advanced models.

By the late 1970s, something else—beyond how to apply basic and advanced economic, philosophical and psychological concepts and develop models or tools from them—was becoming clear. Although MBM was comprised of these concepts or mental models, when applied systematically it was much more than simply a sum of the parts. Its power came from ensuring that each part reinforces and leverages the others. While applying a single dimension, such as incentives, can be beneficial, the lack of a holistic approach results in the loss of much of MBM's power.

As the company continued to grow, our knowledge and talent pool were becoming increasingly large and dispersed. As a result, I was only able to work with or mentor a decreasing percentage of our employees. In turn, our ability to apply these concepts to achieve results diminished while our opportunity to benefit from them increased. We needed to find ways to teach the theory and practice of our concepts and mental models on a much larger scale.

In the early 1980s, we tried to overcome this problem by incorporating our economic thinking and mental models into an existing management system. We thought this would be an efficient way to better connect employees with our philosophy, mental models and resulting tools. The system we selected was that of W. Edwards Deming. Deming's work helped us systematize our focus on one aspect of MBM—continuous improvement. By using Pareto charts, root-cause analysis and statistical process control, we sought to measure our progress in clear and meaningful ways.

## DEMING ON CONTINUOUS IMPROVEMENT

W. Edwards Deming, in emphasizing the need for continuous improvement, said: "You never get out of this hospital."[9]

While we made progress, we also learned valuable lessons. One was that concepts and tools must be used only when they improve results. This point was driven home for me on a mid-1980s trip to the electrical shop at our gas liquids plant in Medford, Oklahoma. The electricians there were spending a large portion of their time measuring activity and drawing charts instead of doing electrical work. Our people referred to this as "charts for Charles." Many employees thought I wanted charts or descriptions of activity as an end in itself, rather than a means to improve results. Unfortunately, measurement and chart-drawing became the focus rather than improving performance and eliminating waste.

We also learned we could not simply graft economic principles and our mental models onto an existing management system, even one as good as Deming's. The problem, as my trip to Medford illustrated, was that we had not provided sufficient understanding of our concepts to enable them to be used to get results. To a person with only a hammer and no understanding, every problem looks like a nail.

This failed experiment with the Deming method helped us better understand how to measure a business's key drivers, analyze problems and eliminate waste. It also caused us to systematically articulate our own framework so our people could integrate theory and practice. The results of proper integration and application are far beyond what can be achieved with either theory or practice alone.

The first step in codifying our own framework was coming up with a name. I hit on Market-Based Management in 1990. I felt this name best reflected the influence of market principles and the need to provide a coherent management philosophy and practice. The challenge, given the differences between a country and an organization, was to discover or develop the mechanisms that would enable us to harness the power of the market economy within the company.

To facilitate the development of these mechanisms, we established the Koch Development Group. We expected this team of internal trainers and consultants to help employees understand and apply our concepts and mental models to achieve results.

At its inception, the Development Group had no products or services to sell. Developing valued services from MBM required synthesizing theory and practice, a codification of the mental models and tools that would best enable our businesses to achieve superior results. We researched the key aspects of a market economy that would enable us to further develop our framework. Teams were formed to examine the role of property rights, rules of just conduct, values, culture, vision, measurement, incentives and knowledge creation in contributing to prosperity.

A problem with the Development Group was the excessive focus of some team members on theory, without understanding how to apply it. Theoretical grounding is necessary, but by itself is not sufficient to obtain results. Besides, our primary need at this point was not more theory, but to develop personal knowledge in order to learn how to profitably apply theory.

## PERSONAL KNOWLEDGE

Chemist and philosopher of science Michael Polanyi argued that we only truly know something—that is, have personal knowledge—when we can apply it to get results. Riding a bike, playing golf or chess are good examples. Personal knowledge, or true understanding, involves converting conceptual knowledge into an effective tool for solving problems, handling new subjects and making discoveries.

Developing personal knowledge involves a personal transformation. It requires learning a new framework and mental models, and then using them to work out concrete problems. Personal knowledge is the result of integrating theory and practice. It can be facilitated by the tutelage of a mentor, such as a painting instructor or golf pro.

Personal knowledge is the key to making discoveries. As we study a particular field, we absorb increasing amounts of specific knowledge, including rules, facts, terminology and relationships. At some point, we know these details well enough that we can begin to focus on the whole. We can then begin to see patterns, the meaning of things, and sense when something is wrong, even though we may not always be able to articulate our understanding. This improves our ability to perceive problems and opportunities when doing research, interviewing a candidate or screening acquisitions.

The process of discovery begins when we observe, often vaguely, a gap between what is and what could be. Our intuition tells us something better is just beyond the range of our mind's eye. To build a culture of discovery, we must encourage, not discourage, the passionate pursuit of our own and others' hunches. Next, we need to strive to clearly articulate our hypotheses, which, when made concrete and specific, can be challenged and tested. Hypotheses that pass this hurdle can then be put to the broader test of working in practice. The genesis of this entire process is the development of personal knowledge that is passionately applied to solve a problem.

Other team members had little or no understanding of the theory, so they too were unable to teach employees how to apply the concepts to achieve results. Consequently, the concepts became little more than buzzwords. Employees used them to justify what they were already doing, or worse, what they wanted to do. Learning how to overcome the tendency for form to take precedence over substance was a key to getting results from MBM.

Still another problem, also caused by poor understanding, was a tendency to apply MBM as a rigid formula. Defining the particulars and prescribing exactly how MBM should be applied undermines the ability to use it to achieve superior results. Recognizing and resisting this natural tendency to bureaucratize everything has been another important step forward.

We are now better at detecting and dealing with such tendencies. In order to fully capture the power of MBM, an organization must not only avoid unproductive tendencies, but continually strive to improve its ability to internalize and apply proper mental models. This requires the most difficult and painful of all changes: A change in the way we think. Accomplishing such a change involves a focused and prolonged effort to develop new habits of thinking based on these mental models. Success in applying new mental models comes only after frequent practice.

To its credit, the Development Group pioneered internal markets and greatly expanded the use of scorecards. This helped us more fully appreciate the value of having measures based on economic reality. It reminded us that, to guide activity correctly, we must measure what leads to results, not simply what is easy to measure. For example, if an evaluation of an employee's performance only includes his or her contribution to current profits but not the effect on long-term profits and culture, we inadvertently encourage employees to work on the wrong things.

While the Development Group no longer exists (its current incarnation is the Koch Industries MBM Capability), its formation was an important step in our attempts to educate employees and codify our business philosophy.

Around 1995, a breakthrough came with the MBM Toolkit, which demonstrated that the five dimensions must be in harmony and applied holistically. From this Toolkit came the MBM Problem-Solving Process, which greatly improved our ability to solve problems and innovate. This success fed on itself because it demonstrated to skeptics the power of the MBM framework. As a result, more people became willing to undertake what Polanyi called the "self-modifying act of conversion"[10] necessary to put a new way of thinking into practice, in this case applying MBM to get results.

## PRACTICING MBM IN A POLITICAL WORLD

From the 1960s through the 1980s, Koch Industries grew through the application of market-based principles. However, just as we were articulating and codifying the system that was contributing to our success, we were caught unprepared by the rapid increase in regulation, politicization and litigation. We were not alone in this regard. These changes have universally damaged the ability of businesses to create real value and contribute to societal well-being.

While business was becoming increasingly regulated, we kept thinking and acting as if we lived in a pure market economy. The reality was far different. The laws of economics seemed less and less relevant in a world where the uncertainty of politics had replaced the uncertainty of the marketplace.

This reality required us to make a cultural change. We needed to be uncompromising, to expect 100 percent of our employees to comply 100 percent of the time with complex and ever-changing government mandates. Striving to comply with every law does not mean agreeing with every law. But, even when faced with laws we think are counter-productive, we must first comply. Only then, from a credible position, can we enter into a dialogue with regulatory agencies to demonstrate alternatives that are more beneficial. If these efforts fail, we can then join with others in using education and/or political efforts to change the law.

The impetus toward regulation and litigation was fueled, in part, by the growing perception that large companies were a collection of schemers who, rather than contributing to prosperity, were using dishonest means and the political and legal systems to unjustly enrich themselves. The recent spectacular failure of several large companies, caused by a lack of humility and integrity among their leaders, only reinforced this perception. We believe the proper application of MBM offers an antidote to these problems.

## ECONOMIC VS. POLITICAL MEANS

Franz Oppenheimer clearly distinguished the "two fundamentally opposed means"[11] by which people obtain resources to satisfy their desires. The first is the economic means: producers creating value. The second is the political means: predators perpetrating legal or illegal plunder.

The economic means of profiting involves voluntarily exchanging your goods or services for the goods or services of others. Parties will not voluntarily enter into an exchange unless they both believe they will be better off. Therefore, you can only profit over time in a system of voluntary exchange (a market) by making others better off.

The political means of profiting transfers goods or services from one party to another by force or fraud. A coerced or fraudulent exchange leaves at least one of the parties worse off. Examples are stealing, committing fraud, polluting, using unsafe practices, filing baseless lawsuits, lobbying governments to hamper competitors or obtain subsidies and promoting self-serving redistribution programs.

The economic means creates wealth by making each participant, and, therefore, society as a whole, better off. The political means, at best, merely redistributes wealth. As a general system, it causes the overwhelming majority of people to be worse off.

Society certainly has the power to enact laws. But for these laws to contribute to prosperity rather than undermine it, they must, among other things, be applied equally to all. A company should not be exempt from environmental emissions laws because it is small or favored politically. We believe that to have a free and prosperous society, people must be treated according to their individual merits, not by group association. Likewise, all businesses should be equal before the law and not treated differently because of size, profitability, industry or political influence. In today's world it is not sufficient to satisfy customers. A company's reputation is critical to how it will be treated by others and to its long-term success. We must build a positive reputation based on reality, or others will create one for us based on speculation or animus and we won't like what they create. A positive reputation is built by behaving consistently with sound principles, creating real value, achieving compliance excellence and living up to commitments. Then the facts about real performance should be communicated. Doing this, as opposed to using gimmicks or false advertising, is the key to building a positive long-term reputation.

This approach also enables an organization to build beneficial relationships and trust with people from all walks of life who share its values—those who are producers, not predators. To maintain these relationships requires that all employees act in a principled manner. Doing so not only enables a company to stay in business, but gives it the opportunity to work with well-meaning people in all levels of government to enact reality-based policies that promote prosperity for the benefit of all.

The table on the following pages summarizes the application of the Science of Human Action in society (the Science of Liberty), in an organization (MBM) and by an individual. Chapters 3–7 provide a detailed examination of each of the five dimensions of MBM.

| APPLICATION | VISION | VIRTUE AND TALENTS |
|---|---|---|
| **THE SCIENCE OF LIBERTY:** How societies can best achieve long-term peace, civility and prosperity. | A system of spontaneous order that maximizes choice, creating sustainable prosperity and societal progress. | Beneficial rules of just conduct—the rule of law and norms of behavior—understood and committed to by the public. |
| **MBM:** How organizations can best survive, prosper and grow long-term. | Determine where and how the organization can best create value in society to maximize its own value long-term through a process of experimental discovery. | Ensure that people with the right virtue and talents are hired and retained. Maintain a culture based on the MBM Guiding Principles. |
| **INDIVIDUAL PERFORMANCE:** How individuals can best develop, contribute and fulfill their potential. | Understand your goals and comparative advantages and how to create the greatest value for yourself, your organization and society. | Understand and consistently act in harmony with the MBM Guiding Principles. |

| KNOWLEDGE PROCESSES | DECISION RIGHTS | INCENTIVES |
|---|---|---|
| Free speech and market signals (prices, profit and loss) based on sound rules and property rights. | Clear, dependable property rights earned according to the value created and comparative advantage. | People benefit through profit and loss according to the value they create in society. |
| Ensure knowledge is optimally acquired, shared and applied. Measure profitability wherever practical. | Ensure the right people are in the right roles with the right authorities. Employees know what they are responsible for and are held accountable. | Employees are rewarded according to the value they create for the organization. |
| Seek and share knowledge and determine what is profitable. Constantly innovate and learn through experimental discovery. | Seek those roles and acquire the necessary resources where you have a comparative advantage. | Do what you have a passion for and is most rewarding to you. |

*"Einstein went on to generalize his vision further and to derive from it a series of new and surprising consequences."*

Michael Polanyi[1]

# CHAPTER 3

# VISION

*"Where there is no vision, the people perish."*

—Proverbs 29:18

*"Columbus cherished a vision of another world,
and he discovered it; Copernicus fostered the vision
of a multiplicity of worlds and a wider universe,
and he revealed it; Buddha beheld the vision
of a spiritual world of stainless beauty
and perfect peace, and he entered into it."*

—James Allen[2]

An effective business vision begins and ends with value creation, which is the only reason any business should exist. In a true market economy, for a business to survive and prosper long term it must develop and use its capabilities to create real, sustainable, superior value for its customers and for society.

## VALUE CREATION

Successful companies create value by providing products or services their customers value more highly than available alternatives. They do this while consuming fewer resources, leaving more resources available to satisfy other needs in society. Value creation involves making people's lives better. It is contributing to prosperity in society.

Value creation is the role of business in a market economy. Businesses that don't create value are not enhancing people's lives. In fact, businesses that destroy value are detrimental to our lives. When businesses make unprofitable products, they are drawing resources away from higher-valued uses, and when businesses waste resources, they prevent them from being beneficially used at all. In either case, a business with unattractive returns should be restructured, sold to a better owner or shut down.

The long-term success of a business is determined by how much it is contributing to improving people's lives and prosperity through value creation. In a true free market, with beneficial rules and property rights, the appropriate measure of the enterprise's value creation is long-term profitability.[3]

Creating superior value means generating greater value from the resources consumed than alternate uses. By resources, we mean not only capital and raw materials, but also labor, intellectual property and other inputs. Superior value can be created by converting these resources into a product or service that has greater value to the customer or by consuming fewer or lower opportunity cost resources to provide the product or service. For example, Koch companies turn crude oil into products such as gasoline, and chemicals into fibers used in carpets and clothes. If we can make these products using fewer or less costly raw materials, the resources saved are available to satisfy other needs, enabling our profits to increase even when our prices decline. If all this is done in harmony with sound principles, we are generating real value in society by the economic means.

The ability of a business to create value is greatly facilitated by a market economy that coordinates the various interests of a diverse population. We all tend to pursue our own interests, but in a true market economy we can only prosper by providing others with what they value. The economist Adam Smith summed up this process when he said: "It is not from the benevolence of the butcher, the brewer, or the baker that we expect our dinner, but from their regard to their own self-interest."[4]

## SELF-INTEREST

By self-interest, Smith meant what Tocqueville called enlightened self-interest, in which people benefit themselves by benefiting others. "Americans are fond of explaining almost all the actions of their lives by the principle of interest rightly understood; they show with complacency how an enlightened regard for themselves constantly prompts them to assist each other."[5]

Such mutual self-interest is best served in a system in which beneficial rules of exchange are enforced. As Vernon Smith has noted, these rules are "the right of possession, its transference by consent, and the performance of promises."[6] This system encourages profiting by the economic means and discourages profiting by the political means.

It is not a question of whether there should be self-interest; it is a question of how to channel that self-interest. "No individual could survive in a world of scarce resources without a strong measure of self-interest, one that includes at the very least his own family and close associates. That self-interest can manifest itself in one of two ways when dealing with strangers; through either aggression or cooperation."[7] For a society or organization to prosper long term it must have rules and incentives that enable and reward enlightened self-interest benefiting others—cooperation—while prohibiting and punishing destructive self-interest that undermines prosperity—aggression.

Even with all of us seeking our own self-interest and even without any society-wide planning, order emerges. Because this emerging order is not centrally planned, F. A. Hayek described it as a spontaneous order. In a market economy, producers and consumers have many alternatives and choices. The fact that new products and methods are constantly driving out old ones presents businesses with constantly changing challenges and opportunities.

## SPONTANEOUS ORDER

Scholars such as Adam Smith and F. A. Hayek have demonstrated that prosperity can only take place through spontaneous order, an order that is the result of human action but not of human design. Adam Smith described this as the "invisible hand" by which, in the proper system, man is led "to promote an end which is no part of his intentions."[8] Hayek argued that prosperity requires that the knowledge dispersed throughout society be put to productive use and that it "cannot be gathered and conveyed to an authority charged with the task of deliberately creating order."[9] Rather, dispersed knowledge can only be put to productive use through a system of spontaneous order based on private property, rules of just conduct (including the rule of law) and free markets. Michael Polanyi believed that science advances through a similar spontaneous order which he called the Republic of Science.

## EMBRACING CHANGE

Given the realities of creative destruction and spontaneous order, how is a business to choose which opportunities to pursue? It does so by developing a vision that guides it in how to create superior value for society. We know a business is being guided by an effective vision to the extent it creates profit over the long term. History has shown that an organization that is continually profitable is satisfying people's needs. Those that are not satisfying needs tend to die out. Remember the *Forbes* listing of successful companies mentioned in Chapter 2? Most of the 100 largest U.S. companies in 1917 had fallen off the list after seven decades and many had disappeared altogether. Why? Because they did not continue to create value for society and therefore failed to generate sufficient profits. They did less and less for society as time went on. We require a vision that guides us to do more and more.

The development of an effective vision begins by recognizing the ways in which an organization can create superior value for society. A vision statement is the organization's view of how it plans to create that value. It should be based on a realistic assessment of its capabilities (as well as improvements it needs to make and the new ones it needs to add) and on a detailed analysis to determine the opportunities for which these capabilities can create the most value. This vision should guide everything the organization does.

A company's vision should take into consideration the fact that, over time, competition erodes the profitability of every product or innovation. Competitors are constantly seeking less costly methods of production and superior new products that destroy the profitability of established products. This is Schumpeter's process of creative destruction.

To maximize profit over the life of a product, a business must slow down the inevitable erosion in the profitability of its products and continually renew or replace them. The wide range of strategies available to slow this decline include: developing good customer relationships; maintaining a strong brand with the quality and consistency to back it up; developing hard-to-duplicate distribution channels; establishing advantaged long-term sales or supply contracts; developing new applications;

protecting intellectual property by using patents, secrecy and contracts; and improving the quality/cost relationship more rapidly than competitors.

The world never stands still. As writer George Will has reminded us: "The future has a way of arriving unannounced."[10] Competitors are constantly improving and what customers value is constantly changing. No matter how superior a company's products and services, it cannot stay in business unless it makes improvements and innovations at least as fast as its competitors. To do this successfully requires that a business apply the processes of experimental discovery and creative destruction to its vision, strategies, products, services and methods. All businesses must constantly innovate.

## EXPERIMENTAL DISCOVERY

F. A. Hayek explained the need for experimental discovery: "The solution of the economic problem is a voyage of exploration into the unknown, an attempt to discover new ways of doing things better. Economic problems are created by unforeseen changes which require adaptation."[11] Since the future is unknown, we can never predict with certainty which investments will be profitable. To drive creative destruction internally, we must maintain numerous well-founded experiments to determine which new products, processes, methods and businesses will be successful. We must also limit the size of these experiments to what can be justified given the risk, the potential and what we can afford to lose.

INVISTA Interiors provides an excellent example of how, through repeated cycles of experimental discovery, creative destruction, innovation and anticipating customer needs, a business can bring about long-term growth. DuPont created and developed the STAINMASTER® carpet business by focusing on the application of its comparative advantage (or core capability) of product and process innovation based on chemistry. As INVISTA's businesses matured and competition increased, additional core capabilities—such as business innovation and operations excellence—were needed to ensure INVISTA's long-term success. Hence DuPont's interest in selling and ours in acquiring INVISTA in 2004.

Leaders of the Interiors business at DuPont knew that to survive and grow they had to renew their products continually. Their original nylon carpet product, although valued for its stain resistance, was made from thick fibers that were rough to the touch. Had the company simply relied on stain resistance to keep the product profitable, it would have lost out to competitors. Indeed, as Figure 4 shows, the original product had a life cycle of about ten years. Subsequent innovations improved softness and introduced other features, such as wear retention and enhanced visual tones, while maintaining its stain-resistant quality. The latest innovations include products with better bulk and softness as well as improved stain and soil resistance. On-going efforts to stay one step ahead of competitors and to anti-cipate what customers will value in the future have fostered continuing innovation.

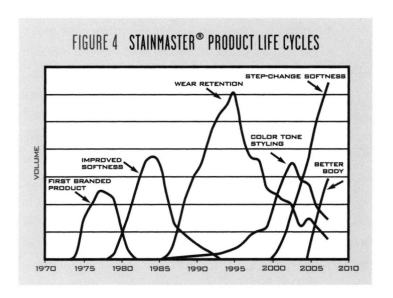

FIGURE 4   STAINMASTER® PRODUCT LIFE CYCLES

Sustained, successful product development requires not only high quality R&D, but also a marketing and manufacturing organization that sees opportunities and has the capability, dis-cipline, integration and culture to capture them. It also requires innovation throughout all of a company's business processes, from supply to manufacturing to marketing, and including human resources, accounting, legal, compliance and other support ser-vices. Koch Industries' strong capabilities in these areas made INVISTA a good fit for us.

## ANTICIPATION AND INNOVATION

Successful product development also requires more than simply responding to customer preferences. Both a company and its customers gain when the company anticipates new value opportunities rather than just reacting to what customers value today. While it is important to ask customers what they will value in the future, the process cannot end there. Focus groups and customer surveys tend to reveal information about tomorrow's needs that are based on today's alternatives. Answers anchored to today's alternatives are likely to be wrong for just that reason. It's difficult to say what you will choose in the future if you don't know what the choices will be.

For example, when large information technology users in the 1970s were asked what computers they would use in the future, 70 percent said IBM® mainframes. But who among us could have imagined the spectacular changes coming in information technology? Certainly not those mainframe users questioned decades ago, many of whom now use $500 personal computers networked via the Internet.

It is natural to think that if customers don't complain, they are satisfied. But thinking this way can lull us into complacency and make us vulnerable to creative destruction. Customers seldom know what they will value until they see it. This essential insight is fundamental to success.

In addition to slowing declines, constantly innovating and anticipating what customers will value, a company must also recognize whether and when to sell an asset or business. In general, an asset should be sold when a buyer will pay more than the owner's estimate of its remaining value. This will tend to be when the rate of decline overcomes the owner's ability to innovate. At Koch Industries, we prefer not to sell assets that provide a core capability or platform for growth.

Naturally, every business wants to receive the most value for something it sells. To do so, it needs to consider the various reasons why an asset or business would be worth more to someone else. A potential purchaser might not believe the business will decline as rapidly. They might see synergies with other complementary assets they own. Or they may have capabilities or innovations the seller does not have. In short, a buyer has a different vision.

How do we create a vision? The development of an effective vision requires recognizing how an organization can create superior value for society and most fully benefit by it. The process starts with a realistic assessment of the business's core capabilities (existing, improved or new) and a preliminary determination of the opportunities for which these capabilities can create the most value. This preliminary determination must be confirmed through the development of a point of view regarding what is going to happen in the industries where the organization believes these opportunities exist.

At Koch Industries overall, we have six core capabilities that have brought about significant, sustainable, competitive advantages: Market-Based Management®, Innovation, Operations

Excellence, Trading, Transaction Excellence and Public Sector. Because these capabilities are critical to KII's future, we are constantly improving and adding to them, building them through theory, observation, practice and measurement. We enhance the application of these capabilities in our businesses through teams in each business, reinforced and supported by a team at the corporate level.

Point of view development involves intensive, systematic, global study. We study the industry's history, technology, competition, customers, applicable laws and barriers to entry, and how all these factors are changing. We then analyze its value chain and cost structure, future demand for its products, competitive positions of participants and other relevant factors. We seek to understand the future drivers and level of profitability for the various segments of the industry.

Based on our point of view, we modify our thinking on the best opportunities and how to capture them. From this analysis, we develop a vision that explicitly states how we plan to create superior value. This vision must be specific enough to guide action and consistent with Koch Industries' vision.

## KOCH INDUSTRIES' VISION

Apply Market-Based Management to identify and capture those opportunities for which our capabilities will create the greatest value and develop and implement strategies that will maximize this value long term. The core capabilities that currently represent our greatest competitive advantages and enable us to create superior value are:

| | |
|---|---|
| MBM | Vision, Virtue and Talents, Knowledge Processes, Decision Rights, Incentives, the Guiding Principles, MBM Models |
| INNOVATION | Creative destruction, disciplined freedom, discovery process, R&D, technology networks, benchmarking, acquisitions, marketing and branding, IP strategy |
| OPERATIONS EXCELLENCE | Compliance, EHS, performance and cost effectiveness, benchmarking, capturing value bets |
| TRADING | Point of view, strategy development, buying and selling assets, optionality, risk management, execution |
| TRANSACTION EXCELLENCE | Opportunity identification, origination network, Decision Making Framework, due diligence, portfolio optimization, structuring |
| PUBLIC SECTOR | Legal, communications, community relations, philanthropy and public policy |

To succeed long term, Koch Industries will continually improve these capabilities and develop additional core capabilities.

The December 2005 purchase of GP illustrates our vision at work. By 2002, we had determined that our core capabilities could create value in the forest products industry and had developed a point of view as to which segments of the industry had the most potential for us. We believed MBM could improve vision development, economic thinking, measures, knowledge creation and sharing, decision making and incentives. Innovation could apply not only in products and processes, but also in all other parts of the value creation process. Operations excellence could improve compliance and cost and performance effectiveness. Trading could improve raw material and energy purchasing, product sales and optionality, and enable us to build a trading business. Transactional excellence could enhance opportunity origination and analysis and financial structuring. Public sector could improve the ability to prevent and defend lawsuits and deal with political and communication challenges. Based on this reasoning, in 2004 we approached GP and subsequently bought two of its pulp mills. Our success with the pulp business encouraged us to seek further opportunities in forest and consumer products and ultimately led to the acquisition of GP.

It is apparent from Koch Industries' vision and the diversity of its businesses that we view ourselves as bounded by capabilities, rather than our industries or products, as is more typical.

At KII, this vision development process applies equally to industries we're in and those we're considering entering. New opportunities exist in our traditional industries just as they do in new ones. Thus, Koch companies apply this same vision development process inside, as well as outside, their current industries. A key part of this process is taking into account the capabilities and appetite for risk of both the business and Koch Industries as a whole.

## SETTING PRIORITIES

Based on its vision, a business needs to develop and implement strategies that will enable it to maximize its long-term value (which we consider to be its long-term profitability above its cost of capital). This requires setting priorities. In a complex business, deciding the order in which to do things can be just as important as deciding what things to do.

At least two sets of criteria are needed to determine priorities. The first set includes those actions that are required to stay in business, such as meeting a deadline for complying with a government regulation or a major customer's quality or volume requirements. The second set is determined by gap analyses that estimate the risk-adjusted present value of the opportunities relative to the resources consumed (such as scarce talent or capital). Thus, an opportunity with a risk-adjusted present value of $100 million will take precedence over one of $20 million, assuming similar resources are required. Without such a methodology, the tendency is to try to work on everything at once, which means nothing gets done quickly or well.

After priorities are set for the business as a whole, based on the vision, they must also be set for marketing, operations (down to the plant level), supply, R&D and the support groups. Each must then assign responsibility for executing these priorities. Opportunity cost must be considered in deciding what to do and in what order.

Maximizing long-term value also involves creating an experimental discovery process that encourages new improvements, strategies and innovations. When we are experimenting, we will have failures. As Einstein taught: "Someone who has never made a mistake has never tried anything new."[12] The key is to recognize when we are experimenting and to develop a vision based on reality. KII has been hurt when we failed to do so.

Our losses in shipping and agriculture were costly examples of the failure to develop a reality-based vision and recognize that we did not have the capability to make bets of such complexity or magnitude. Both are profitable today, but only after being completely reconstituted. New capabilities have been built, resulting in revised visions. For example, two very successful businesses, Koch Nitrogen and the Matador Cattle Co., were part of the failed Koch Agriculture Group. Koch Nitrogen's realization of its revised vision as a global fertilizer company that operates, markets and trades was made possible by the consistent, disciplined application of Market-Based Management. That same approach also allowed the Matador Cattle Co. to make its revised vision a reality.

For an established organization, vision development is seldom a linear process. Instead, the process is iterative and the vision is in a state of continual emergence. Once established, every vision contains the seeds of its own demise. Creative destruction will see to that.

Even though a vision will change over time, it is essential to have a shared vision that is understood and embraced. Thus, the vision must be effectively communicated throughout the organization. Understanding what the business is trying to achieve and how it creates value helps each employee focus and prioritize. A shared vision guides the development of roles, responsibilities and expectations. Every vision should answer the questions, "What should we be striving to do?" and "How will we do it?" Our vision must guide all our actions. An effective vision is the genesis of long-term success.

*"There is a natural aristocracy among men. The grounds of this are virtue and talents."*

Thomas Jefferson[1]

# CHAPTER 4

# VIRTUE AND TALENTS

*"Laws control the lesser man.*
*Right conduct controls the greater one."*
—Chinese proverb

*"The greatest virtues are those*
*which are most useful to other persons."*
—Aristotle[2]

The need for talent is obvious. However, as Thomas Jefferson noted, virtue is at least as important as talent. To be a truly successful organization, one that excels and stands the test of time, virtue as well as talent must be emphasized. At Koch Industries, we do this by embracing certain core values in our company that perform the role F. A. Hayek's "rules of just conduct" play in society. These core values are incorporated in our MBM® Guiding Principles and our Code of Conduct.

## RULES OF JUST CONDUCT

In society, rules of just conduct encompass both the rule of law and norms of behavior. Rules of just conduct are not a specific set of rules. Rather, they are a general standard by which all laws can be measured.

The rule of law bounds government power and limits its authority to change laws arbitrarily, even when desired by the majority. It also implies that laws must be applied consistently to all, and that all are equal before the law. The rule of law ensures equality of treatment (not equality of outcome), individual freedom and discretion. These lead to civility, prosperity and societal progress. The rule of law, properly applied, secures individual rights, makes the political world more predictable, enables individuals to more easily adapt and leads to behavior that is beneficial to society.

Norms of behavior are how we behave and expect others to behave. For a free society to function, beneficial norms of behavior, such as honesty, respect for others and their property, making a contribution, being responsible and taking initiative must be widely practiced. Norms of behavior, when combined with shared values and beliefs—what is deeply cared about— comprise a group's culture.

To function effectively, any group of people, whether a society or an organization, must be guided largely by general rules of just conduct, not specific commands. Leaving the particulars to the person doing the work encourages discovery. It also enhances adaptation to changing conditions.

When detailed rules or instructions are necessary, they must be judged against those general rules already established through a process of discovery as best enabling a society or organization to prosper. Over-specifying and enforcing particulars undermines prosperity by encouraging inaction. It also facilitates corruption and abuse of power, subservience and stagnation. As the French writer Frederic Bastiat put it,

"... the surest way to have the laws respected is to make them respectable."[3]

Our MBM Guiding Principles articulate our rules of just conduct along with our shared values and beliefs. Enforcing general principles enables employees to challenge the particulars. To the extent that particulars are enforced, the general breaks down.

Every one of us must internalize these core values and exemplify them in all we do. We call this Principled Entrepreneurship™, by which we maximize value creation.

## PRINCIPLED ENTREPRENEURSHIP

Principled Entrepreneurship is maximizing long-term profitability for the business by creating real value in society while always acting lawfully and with integrity.

## A CULTURE OF VIRTUE

Every organization has its own culture. It may be created intentionally by the organization or inadvertently by other forces. In either case, an organization's culture is determined by the conduct of its members and the rules set by its leaders and governments. MBM requires a culture that has specific attributes. Fortunately, these attributes can be actively cultivated. They set the standards for evaluating policies and practices, measuring conduct, establishing norms of behavior and building the shared values that guide individual actions.

## MBM GUIDING PRINCIPLES

1. INTEGRITY: Conduct all affairs lawfully and with integrity.
2. COMPLIANCE: Strive for 10,000% compliance, with 100% of employees fully complying 100% of the time. Ensure excellence in environmental, safety, and all other areas of compliance. Stop, think, and ask.
3. VALUE CREATION: Create real, long-term value by the economic means. Understand, develop, and apply MBM to achieve superior results. Eliminate waste.
4. PRINCIPLED ENTREPRENEURSHIP: Demonstrate the sense of urgency, discipline, accountability, judgment, initiative, economic and critical thinking skills, and the risk-taking mentality necessary to generate the greatest contribution to the company and society.
5. CUSTOMER FOCUS: Understand and develop relationships with customers to profitably anticipate and satisfy their needs.
6. KNOWLEDGE: Seek and use the best knowledge and proactively share your knowledge while embracing a challenge process. Measure profitability wherever practical.
7. CHANGE: Embrace change. Envision what could be, challenge the status quo, and drive creative destruction.

8. HUMILITY: Practice humility and intellectual honesty. Constantly seek to understand and constructively deal with reality to create real value and achieve personal improvement.

9. RESPECT: Treat others with dignity, respect, honesty, and sensitivity. Appreciate the value of diversity. Encourage and practice teamwork.

10. FULFILLMENT: Produce results that create value to realize your full potential and find fulfillment in your work.

Developing the ability to apply these Principles routinely and instinctively to achieve results requires constant practice and reflection.

Many companies have similar principles, but fewer take systematic steps to ensure that every employee understands and is committed to thinking and acting in harmony with them. These steps are essential if such principles are to truly affect workplace culture. Otherwise, they are nothing more than empty slogans.

The first step is to ensure that policies and practices lead to a culture of value creation, initiative and responsibility rather than one of bureaucracy, entitlement and unaccountability. At KII, we also strive to hire and retain only those who embrace our Principles. We provide detailed explanations of these Principles and their role, and then clearly and consistently communicate the expectation that our Principles guide employee behavior. In addition, we base advancement and compensation on how well our employees practice our Principles. We also provide regular feedback and will discipline and ultimately terminate employees who do not act in harmony with our Principles.

Leaders should be selected from among those employees who have demonstrated competence in the execution of these steps and are positive role models for workplace culture. Because leaders set the standard, both by how they lead and by what they do, they are the guardians of culture and are held accountable for it. To be effective, leaders must internalize and consistently apply sound principles in a way that produces results.

For MBM to be applied effectively, results must be the focus. The challenge is to get beyond the glib stage in which employees understand the words and concepts but haven't yet been able to apply them to achieve profitable results. Promoting those who cannot "walk the talk" undermines the ability to create value and damages culture. One knows chess, by analogy, when one can apply the concepts and basic rules to create winning strategies. A key talent for management positions is the ability to read people and identify those who are able to apply sound principles to achieve profitable results.

Creating a beneficial culture requires mentoring and positive examples. In addition to living by these principles, good leaders regularly review them with all employees. Effective leaders provide frequent and honest feedback that identifies opportunities for improvement in a way that stimulates dialogue and change. They hold themselves, their employees, peers and management accountable for behavior in keeping with these principles. Leaders also provide opportunities for employees who best exemplify a beneficial workplace culture. Such employees focus on core business issues, drive constructive change, innovate and achieve profitable results and growth through Principled Entrepreneurship.

The ability to create real value depends on a principled, entrepreneurial culture in which the members are passionate about discovery. Although employees are selected and retained on the basis of their values and beliefs, they must also have the necessary talent to produce results. Virtue without the required talent does not create value. But talent without virtue is dangerous and can put the company and other employees at risk. Employees with insufficient virtue have done far more damage to companies than those with insufficient talent. Several years ago, a supervisor in one of our plants decided—even after training—that a new government requirement wasn't beneficial. He saw no need to comply with it. We self-reported his violation and also terminated the employee. Both virtue (that is, living by our shared values and beliefs) and talent (the specific skills and knowledge required to excel in a specific role) must be present.

## TALENTS

The potential of each of us to develop specific skills and knowledge is determined by our individual intelligences. There are a number of different kinds of intelligence, and none of us is equally gifted or deficient in all of them. This is why it is important to build diverse teams and organizations with an eye toward the right combinations of talent.

We strive to select, reward and provide opportunities for individuals who create or have the potential to create the most value. This is why we appreciate the value of diversity. A truly free society rewards people according to their individual merits, not by what group they are associated with. Similarly, organizations applying MBM reward people according to their virtue and their contributions. We strive to find those who can create the most value through a diversity of perspectives, experience, knowledge and abilities. Diversity within a company is also important to help it better understand and relate to its customers and communities in this diverse world.

## MULTIPLE INTELLIGENCES

This theory, developed by Howard Gardner, suggests that we each have several independent forms of intelligence.[4] Rarely, if ever, does someone rate high or low on all of them. Each intelligence entails the capacity for learning, solving problems and creating products or services of value to others.

Gardner identified at least eight different kinds of intelligence, each with several subtypes or varieties. While all eight are important in society, two—musical and bodily-kinesthetic—are less relevant to KII. In brief, the other six are:

## INTERPERSONAL:

This intelligence is used in understanding other people, recognizing their virtue and talents, what motivates them and how to work cooperatively with them. It involves the ability to notice and make distinctions among others and getting them to cooperate with each other. Leaders, sales people and teachers need high degrees of this intelligence.

## INTRAPERSONAL:

This is interpersonal intelligence turned inward. It is the capacity to continually, accurately and realistically self-assess in order to operate effectively in life. This keen awareness of one's own intelligences, motivations and feelings is critical for leaders. Those who are weak in this dimension can cause untold damage to themselves and others. This is especially true of those who become completely disconnected from self-reality.[5]

## LINGUISTIC:

The hallmark of this intelligence is a sensitivity to the meaning of words, their order, sounds, rhythms and inflections. It includes the ability to convince others of a course of action and to communicate ideas meaningfully and effectively. It enables the use of language to learn and teach, to draw different or deeper meanings out of statements or works of others and to secure useful information by skillful questioning or discussion. These abilities are central to the effectiveness of anyone who speaks, writes, learns or challenges, such as students, teachers, leaders, speakers, authors, sales people and lawyers.

## LOGICAL-MATHEMATICAL:

The nonverbal ability to construct solutions to logical, mathematical and scientific problems, to solve problems by using measurement, logic and calculation, and to see patterns. It includes the ability to determine what has happened and what may happen in different scenarios, to make economic calculations and to analyze ventures. It involves both deductive and inductive reasoning as well as discerning relationships and connections. Individuals who formulate, analyze, research, innovate, calculate or challenge need to be strong in this intelligence.

## SPATIAL:

The kind of intelligence necessary to form a mental model of a three-dimensional world and to maneuver and operate using that model. It involves being able to perceive the spatial world accurately, to visualize in space and to perform transformations and modifications on these perceptions. This is exhibited both by those who deal directly with the spatial world, such as designers and engineers, and those who apply spatial tools in their work, such as traders and chemists who depict three-dimensional relationships.

## NATURALIST:

The ability to make distinctions in the natural world between plants, animals, clouds, rock formations, etc. It draws on pattern-detecting capacities that enabled our ancestors to survive. It involves perceiving objects through one of the senses, making distinctions about those objects and then classifying them according to specific criteria. In the industrial world, this intelligence is important for those who prepare foods, construct buildings, mine ores or protect the environment. It is also necessary for those who need to distinguish between products, brands, raw materials, etc.

Intelligence is defined as a person's absolute potential in each of these areas. We all have some ability in each, but there are wide variations in which of our abilities are high or low. This is one reason why comparative advantages always exist among any combination of individuals.

For our purposes, Gardner's model need not be exactly correct, only directionally correct. What is important is recognizing the fundamental variance among individuals.

Selection begins with a clear vision of the role in question and the talent necessary to carry out that role.[6] The selection process, like everything else, is subject to challenge and modification. It operates, evolves and improves through interaction and discovery, and is facilitated by an approval process based on comparative advantage.

In thinking about a candidate's suitability for a particular role or an employee's performance, consider the following matrix:

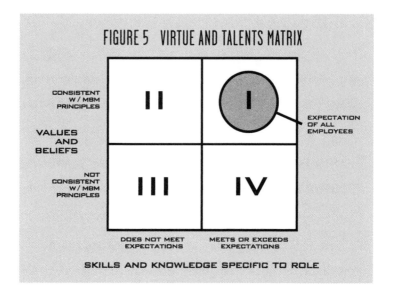

FIGURE 5   VIRTUE AND TALENTS MATRIX

Note that the Values and Beliefs axis is not designated "high-low" or "good-bad." It can, however, be used as an aid in evaluating whether a person fits in an organization. This matrix also facilitates discussion and knowledge-sharing among interviewers, enabling them to better assess candidates.

We expect all employees, as well as candidates, to demonstrate harmony with the values and beliefs expressed in our MBM Guiding Principles. Employees also must have the potential to build the requisite skills and knowledge to meet or exceed the expectations of their positions. Quadrant I in Figure 5 does not identify a superstar—it identifies expectations. Obviously, many employees new to a role will initially be in Quadrant II, but this should be a temporary situation. An employee who, for whatever reason, is not in Quadrant I is expected to get there quickly.

Because we want Koch Industries to succeed over the long term, we cannot afford to select or retain individuals whose core values are inconsistent with our MBM Guiding Principles. If there are doubts surrounding a candidate, they must be resolved. If an existing employee's values are inconsistent with our Principles, action must be taken.

## EMPLOYEE DEVELOPMENT

Development is a continuous improvement process that occurs at both the organizational and individual level. At the organizational level, leaders must actively manage the overall talent mix. Effective leaders recognize the need to fill key positions with individuals who have a competitive advantage in performing their roles when compared with their peers across that industry. Both to develop the vision and to ensure the organization has the talent to make it a reality, leaders rate their employees' performance at an A, B or C level.

## ABC PROCESS

**A level:** Employees whose performance and contribution in their current roles provide significant competitive advantage over those employees in similar roles at principal competitors and, therefore, are exceptional contributors to long-term profitability. These employees are usually among the top 15 percent of their peers throughout the industry in their current role. A business should ensure it doesn't lose them. KII is constantly in the market for A-level employees and must continually improve its ability to identify and recruit these competitively advantaged individuals.

**B level:** Employees whose performance and contribution in their current roles have proven to be at least as good as that of their peers at principal competitors. They tend to be between the top 15th and 50th percent of performers throughout the industry in their current roles. B's are solid contributors who consistently meet expectations and who may exceed expectations in many areas of performance. B-level employees are, collectively, critical to a company's success. They are not an afterthought, living in the shadow of A performers. However, they should be challenged to grow and improve.

**C level:** Employees whose performance and contribution in their current roles put us at a competitive disadvantage by being below-average relative to their peers at principal competitors. C-level employees are not meeting expectations. They may be in the wrong role, meaning they could contribute at a B or even an A level if they were in a role that better leveraged their comparative advantages. But if their performance cannot be improved to a B level, either by finding a suitable role or through development, they should not be retained.

Inability to create value at one company does not mean the same will be true elsewhere. Employees may be much more successful in another organization that has needs or a culture better suited to their talents and values.

The purpose of the ABC process is to determine and improve the level of talent, and to ensure that all employees are in optimum roles and contributing to profitability. The last is achieved by the development of existing employees, the reassignment or termination of underperforming employees and the recruitment of outstanding external talent. Much of this assessment is qualitative and based on judgment because performance can't always be measured and compared with precision. This process should not be applied as a bureaucratic, rigid formula. Rather, it is simply a tool to help leaders acquire, develop and maintain the talent required to advance their vision. Furthermore, employee performance will change over time. Some employees greatly improve their performance, while the performance of others may deteriorate because of their inability to adapt to a changing environment or other factors. For a business to create value in society, its employees must create value for the business. Any employee who is not contributing to value creation is undermining their business's ability to do so. Therefore, any employee who is not creating value does not have a real job in the MBM sense of the word. This philosophy and the ABC process should be applied to all employees— salaried, hourly and temporary—in a way that improves the company's performance.

The initial emphasis of the ABC process should be on C- and A-level employees. Focused strategies should be put in place for C-level employees to improve performance through training, development, mentoring or role change. Employees who do not quickly respond to these efforts and continue to perform at a C level should not be retained. Otherwise, their performance puts other team members and the entire organization at risk. Having the discipline to address C performers enables management to spend the majority of its time ensuring that A performers are fully developed, utilized and challenged, and that B's are given every opportunity to become A's. A's are the mainspring of competitive advantage. The need to continually provide new opportunities for A performers is one reason a company must always be growing.

In addition to constantly developing existing talent from within, new A-level talent from outside the organization must be identified and recruited. This enables a business to build additional competitive advantages, capture more growth opportunities and provide for succession if internal candidates are not available. To maximize long-term profitability, each employee must be committed to sound principles, have the appropriate level and kind of talent and be in the optimum role.

Just as important as selecting talent for the company is selecting who to be in business with. Selecting incompatible partners, whether at the shareholder or the joint venture level, can be as damaging as selecting the wrong employees. Due to the emotions involved, this problem can be even more severe when the partners are family members or friends.

Sixty-some years of experience with dozens of different partners have taught us the importance of partnering with those who share our vision and values. If we find that a partner no longer shares our vision or values, we strive to dissolve the partnership. The longer a deep-seated difference is allowed to fester, the greater the animosity and the more difficult it is to reach an amicable solution.

If partners have conflicting and irreconcilable visions, the business will not realize its potential and will probably fail. If one partner views the business as a cash cow while the other partner's vision is to innovate and grow, the solution is either to sell the business or for one partner to buy out the other. Likewise, if the partners have incompatible values, it will be extremely difficult for the business to succeed long term. Recognizing we rarely have had a successful partnership in which our partners were at odds with our MBM Guiding Principles, we are careful to partner only with those who have similar values.

The worst situation is to be locked into a hostile partnership with no separation mechanism. Such partnerships tend to degenerate into a stalemate in which nothing can be decided and the business atrophies. We had one joint venture in which the partner began vetoing everything we recommended. In an effort to prove how important he was, he also started showing up an hour and a half late for board meetings. Fortunately, our agreement included a divorce procedure that allowed us to gain separation. We don't enter into partnerships without an exit mechanism.

On the other hand, partnerships with a shared vision and values—in which the partners contribute according to their comparative advantages—can be powerful vehicles for superior value creation. Wichita entrepreneur George Ablah, for example, was our partner in ABKO. Thanks to his vision (which we shared) and the values we had in common, we were able to create a very successful real estate partnership that bought Chrysler Realty.

My brother David and I have always shared the same vision for KII: to innovate, grow and reinvest to maximize long-term value by applying our core capabilities in the ways that will create the most value. David has always been objective and fair-minded, making what was best for the company his priority. The same is true of the Marshall family. J. Howard and Pierce Marshall, and Pierce's widow, Elaine, have been resolute allies of ours through bad times as well as good. J. Howard, co-founder of the Great Northern Oil Company, enabled us to gain control of Great Northern by putting his minority interest (which he could have sold to others at a premium) under our control. He had such trust that he did this based on nothing more than our promise we would treat him fairly.

Although it is extremely rare for anyone to display this level of trust, the long-term results demonstrate its power. Trust enables people to accomplish things that would otherwise be impossible and to work efficiently and in harmony toward a common vision. Nobel laureate Kenneth Arrow called trust "an important lubricant of a social system."[7] It is just as important in a business.

*"When Soviet nail factories had their output measured by weight, they tended to make big, heavy nails, even if many of these big nails sat unsold on the shelves while the country was crying out for small nails."*

Thomas Sowell[1]

# CHAPTER 5

# KNOWLEDGE PROCESSES

*"The greatest obstacle to discovery is not ignorance
but the illusion of knowledge."*

—Daniel Boorstin[2]

*"The worth and value of knowledge is in proportion
to the worth and value of its object."*

—Samuel T. Coleridge[3]

Market economies are successful, in large part, because they are superior at creating useful knowledge. The main mechanisms of this knowledge generation are market signals from trade—prices, profit and loss—and free speech.

Societies are most prosperous when knowledge is plentiful, accessible, relevant, inexpensive and growing. Such conditions are most fully brought about by trade.

## TRADE

The foundation of trade is mutual gain. People make exchanges because they expect them to improve their well-being, although sometimes one of the counter-parties is later disappointed. We all tend to be better off when trade is informed and free from force and fraud. The sources of this gain over time are:

- Goods move from those who value them less to those who value them more

- Greater production and consumption and a greater variety of goods and services are made possible by specialization

- Higher volume production by individual producers leads to improved productivity of labor and lower production costs

Throughout history, trade has been a primary determinant of a society's prosperity and progress. Rarely has a great civilization developed in isolation. How conducive a country's geography and politics have been to trade has tended to determine its cultural and economic development. Countries that have had the greatest exposure to and use of goods, knowledge, methods and innovations from all over the world have progressed the earliest and the most. Countries such as Holland and England became trading centers because they were open societies with excellent ports and harbors and thus accessible to ships, the only efficient form of transportation in earlier centuries. Other areas in the world, such as parts of Africa, Central and South America, and Eastern Europe, were isolated by mountains or other geographic or political barriers and did not keep pace.

The same is true for a business. No company, no matter how capable its employees, can match the pace of innovation and improvement taking place throughout the world solely by internal means. Thus, for a company to keep up with its competition and the ongoing changes in technology, methods, markets and what people value, it must quickly develop mechanisms to become aware of relevant developments taking place everywhere in the world. These mechanisms include trading, benchmarking, regular dialogue with specialists, technology origination networks and relationships with knowledgeable business servers.

Knowledge fuels prosperity by signaling and guiding resources to higher-valued uses. Besides enabling producers to develop products that create greater value for consumers, new knowledge also helps producers do so with less resources. The discovery and application of knowledge leads to the improved use, allocation and consumption of resources. Within an organization, knowledge is essential for creating superior value for its customers and the company. A knowledge process is the method by which we develop, supplant, share and apply knowledge to create value.

To succeed in an uncertain future, a company must draw on the knowledge dispersed among its employees.[4] It must also encourage them to discover new ways to create value. Employees must innovate, not just in technology, but in all aspects and at all levels of the business. A market-based knowledge process coordinates dispersed knowledge, applying it at the appropriate time and place to enable the company to profitably satisfy changing needs. Mechanisms for coordinating knowledge are indispensable for bringing about the spontaneous order necessary for creating superior value.

## MEASURES

Critical knowledge is also gained by measuring results. It is often tempting to measure things that are easy to measure; instead, we need to measure those things that matter, even when it is very difficult to do so. As Einstein cautioned: "Not everything that counts can be counted, and not everything that can be counted counts."[5] The most fundamental measures for any business are prices and profit and loss. A business uses them to determine what people value and how best to satisfy those values. In a truly free economy, profit and loss is the market's objective measure of the value a business is creating in society.

To succeed, a business must develop and continually improve profit and loss measures, and determine the underlying drivers, so it can understand what is adding value, what is not, and why. This knowledge informs its vision and strategies, leads to innovations, creates opportunities to eliminate waste and guides continuous improvement. Knowing why something is profitable is often as valuable as knowing what is profitable. This is why a business must also develop measures that help it understand what drives profit.

A successful organization will measure and strive to understand the profitability (and profitability drivers) of its assets, products, strategies, customers, agreements, employees and anything else for which it is practical to do so. One business KII acquired was failing, in part, because it had very few profitability measures. The profitability of plants, products, customers and employees was not measured. We worked with that business to develop measures and found that the 60 percent of the volume of one product sold to a few large customers generated only 20 percent of the profit. The remaining 40 percent, which was sold to many smaller customers, generated 80 percent of the profit. After determining that this condition would continue, the sales team, which had traditionally spent most of its time and effort on the few large customers, began to focus on their smaller, more profitable customers. Measures, as this example illustrates, are critical to understanding where to focus time and resources.

It is also important to understand the rate of change taking place within an industry and whether a business is improving and innovating at a pace that is equal to, or faster than, its competitors. To do this well, it is important to measure trends and compare them to competitors. The rate of change in market share, cost reductions, improvement or deterioration in margins, percentage of revenues from new products, etc., are all examples of such comparisons.

Measures should be quantitative wherever possible, but qualitative and intangible components must also be considered. While it can be difficult to measure value or cost for some things, the attempt to do so often leads to important knowledge. Having the discipline to ask, "What are the key drivers of value and cost?" and "How do we increase profit?" for any given activity is critical to achieving creative insights.

In transforming our Matador Cattle Co.'s Beaverhead Ranch in Montana, a key element was determining and measuring the key drivers of profitability and acting to improve these drivers. Besides costs, the drivers were cattle carrying capacity, calf crop percentage, weaning weights, environmental performance and attracting the right people. By focusing on these, the ranch reduced costs by 25 percent, increased carrying capacity by 8 percent, raised the calf crop from 90 to 95 percent, upped weaning weights by 20 percent, won seven major environmental awards and became the first ranch in the country to be certified by the Wildlife Habitat Council for rebuilding wild animal populations.

In developing measures, accuracy should always be emphasized over precision. It is usually wasteful to develop detailed information beyond what is necessary to make correct decisions. Since it is impossible to predict outcomes precisely, trying to do so is wasteful. Even worse, such attempts can create a false sense of confidence. On the other hand, it is critical to measure real drivers of profitability. For example, energy consumption should be compared to the ideal, not to some budgeted amount.

It is easy to fall into the trap of a single-minded emphasis on cost reduction. Cost is only one component (although a critically important one) of value creation. If your goal is to lose weight, you could accomplish it by cutting off your leg, but that is hardly beneficial. Cost-cutting for its own sake can be just as shortsighted and can seriously damage future profitability. It is more appropriate to focus on eliminating waste, that is, unprofitable activities in light of opportunity cost.

The increasingly global nature of Koch companies provides additional opportunities to eliminate waste. Our John Zink subsidiary, a leading combustion company, recognized it could not simply rely on strong brands to sustain its profitability. This is why it continually seeks to reduce the cost as well as improve the performance of its products. Today, some of John Zink's most complex, labor-intensive components are made in China by a company that specializes in the precision casting of decorative door handles. By looking beyond traditional suppliers, John Zink was able to reduce costs by nearly 50 percent while also greatly improving quality and shortening delivery time.

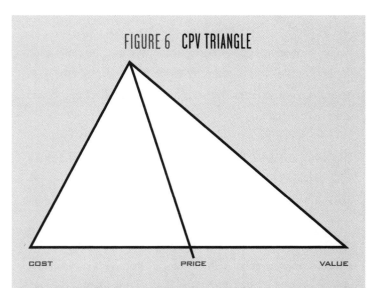

FIGURE 6  **CPV TRIANGLE**

COST                                PRICE                                VALUE

The seller's profit is the difference between the price and the cost to provide a product, while the buyer's profit is the difference between price and the value to the buyer of that same product. Not only does price divide the total value between the seller and buyer, it determines whether there will be a transaction at all. A price below a potential producer's costs usually means no more units of the product will be provided by that producer. If the price is higher than the valuation of a potential buyer, then there will be no transaction and no value will be created for the buyer or the seller.

Michael Porter, the author of *Competitive Strategy*, states that businesses try to gain an advantage by either being the low-cost producer or getting a price premium by differentiating their product. The CPV Triangle helps us understand how to apply both of these approaches.

A cost-advantaged producer focuses on constantly eliminating waste. This is done by examining the profitability of every activity, process, person, resource, product and asset, and by benchmarking.

Product differentiation can be achieved by understanding what customers value now and anticipating what they will value in the future. Based on that understanding, the producer must continually innovate to develop higher-valued products and services than competitors. Creating more value for customers and capturing a share of that value creates a better outcome for both buyers and sellers. It is important to note that customers will value the product according to their subjective values.

Businesses that differentiate their products are less constrained by competitors' actions. Price is no longer solely a lowest common denominator; it is largely determined by how much premium customers are willing to pay for the extra value provided. Generally, a business person should attempt to be a price seeker rather than a price taker. This is best done by discovering new ways of creating value that are difficult to imitate. It is in both the supplier/innovator's and the customer's interest for the innovator to initially capture the majority of this superior value. This provides the incentive for the supplier to continue to innovate, since, given creative destruction, the portion he can capture will decline over time.

There are at least three ways to measure waste or success at eliminating waste. The most direct and obvious way is to examine whether a specific change has improved profitability. For example, if, after cutting costs, profitability drops when other factors have not changed, then we know that what was eliminated was not waste. Designing profitable cost-cutting initiatives involves marginal analysis, economic thinking, critical analysis and sound judgment. It involves determining not only whether something is worth doing, but also how well it is done and if there is a more profitable alternative.

## MARGINAL ANALYSIS

Marginal analysis entails weighing the costs and benefits of a change. We call it marginal not because it is unimportant, but because it is incremental, occurring at the margin. Marginal analysis looks at the benefits and costs associated with a specific change rather than at the average or the whole. It asks, what is the profitability of one more unit of production, of one more plant, or of a larger versus a smaller investment? Before doing marginal analysis we must optimize the current state. For example, before estimating the profitability of an investment to improve efficiency, the current waste should be eliminated from the base case. When considering an expansion, it is wrong to conclude that because we already have excess people we don't need to include the expense of adding any. The economics should be done with the excess people removed from the base case and added to the extent required in the expansion case.

Most decisions should be made using marginal analysis. This requires understanding the difference between costs and benefits that are marginal and those that are not, such as sunk costs. Only by making decisions on the appropriate margin will a business consistently enhance its profitability and eliminate waste.

## BENCHMARKING

Another way to measure and learn to eliminate waste is benchmarking. Benchmarking is the process of identifying, understanding and adapting outstanding practices from anywhere in the world to help us improve. This can be done in several ways. We can learn from the best in the company (internal), the best in the industry (competitive) and the best in the world (world-class). Analyzing the leading company's performance in a specific function, such as maintenance, sales, operations, IT, accounting, etc., is a powerful way to learn how to achieve the best possible results.

Effective benchmarking requires objectivity, so it must be done with humility and intellectual honesty. Such objectivity is sometimes painful, but essential to understanding the gap between performance and best practices and what is necessary to profitably eliminate that gap. When Southwest Airlines sought ways to decrease the time it took to refuel, disembark and board passengers, and unload and load baggage, it did not study other airlines. It studied NASCAR pit crews and drivers. Today, other airlines benchmark themselves against Southwest. Best practices must be sought wherever they are, both inside and outside the company and industry.

## OPPORTUNITY COST

Measuring profitability and benchmarking, while powerful, are not sufficient. Because we are limited in time and resources, pursuing one activity naturally precludes another. Robert Frost recognized this in his famous poem, "The Road Not Taken." When he comes to a fork in the road, Frost realizes that in choosing between the two, the cost of his choice is the one not taken.

The true cost of any activity is the highest-valued activity forgone—that is, the opportunity cost. Working on a profitable activity is wasteful when there is another, even more profitable activity that could be performed instead. It sounds counterintuitive, but profit can be increased by eliminating some profitable, value-adding activities when doing so enables a business to capture higher-valued opportunities. It is essential to learn how to identify this form of waste by rigorously examining all opportunities and alternatives. Waste is eliminated by prioritizing according to profitability, adjusted for risk and time. John Wooden, a basketball coaching legend, summed up opportunity cost–based decision making when he cautioned, "Don't measure yourself by what you have accomplished, but rather by what you should have accomplished with your ability."[6]

Every resource (not just assets and raw materials, but also talent) has alternative uses. Always seek the highest-valued alternative for every resource. Some time ago, the sales representative of the Koch Materials Company (KMC) asphalt plant in Council Bluffs, Iowa, read an article about a company looking for land to build a new casino. Despite the fact this plant had been consistently profitable, he thought, "Would these people place more value on our land and location than we do for producing asphalt?" Upon analysis, KMC determined that the hold value of the asset (the present value of expected future cash flows) was much less than its value as a casino site. There is now an Ameristar Casino and Hotel where the Council Bluffs asphalt plant once stood. The asphalt plant was relocated.

## PROFIT CENTERS

A business can best determine where and how to create value when it is organized into profit centers. Profit centers can be created wherever there are identifiable products, market prices, customers, suppliers and assets such that financial statements can be prepared. These financial statements must reflect economic reality.[7] Remember, anywhere profit and loss is measured, analysis is also needed to understand what drives those results.

Identifying and efficiently creating profit centers at the lowest practical level can provide a substantial competitive advantage. Ideally, each plant should be a profit center and, if it makes more than one product, the profitability of each product should be tracked. When a business sells products or services to external customers, the prices reflect economic reality. When transferring products internally, prices should also reflect the market alternative. As such, the internal price should represent the weighted average market price of the entire volume, not just a portion.

Transferring products using a cost-based system leads to faulty profit signals and bad decisions. Sometimes, restricting our business units to buying internally can be just as wasteful. These profit-distorting practices are especially harmful when they are done to prop up a struggling business or plant. If an operation can't be made profitable, considering its effect on other parts of the company, it must be sold or closed, not subsidized.

The purpose of internal markets is to provide internal signals, so that decision making can be based on this information. This framework ensures decisions are made on the basis of business profitability to the same extent as external purchases. Proper internal markets generate knowledge, guide decisions, reinforce ownership and accountability, encourage entrepreneurship and help eliminate waste.

Profit centers consist not only of the activities necessary to produce, sell and deliver products to an outside customer, but supporting activities, such as accounting and credit services.

Such support services, without oversight, tend to maximize their services rather than maximize their contribution to profitability. To eliminate this problem wherever possible, put these services under the control of the relevant business, or use the internal market or other mechanisms and measures. Measuring the overall economic performance of a profit center is a straightforward task. It is much more difficult to measure the profitability of its internal functions, processes, support services or projects whose possible payoff will come years later. Despite this difficulty, it is important to estimate their profitability by benchmarking or other techniques. The profitability of outsourcing should be measured against the quality-adjusted cost of doing the work internally or having another division or affiliated company do it. The profitability of individual employees should also be estimated. This can be done by tracking, quantitatively where possible, their contributions (positive and negative) through the year and doing an annual 360-degree performance evaluation. Such an evaluation involves getting performance feedback from those who worked most closely with the individual during the year—supervisors, peers and subordinates.

## FREE SPEECH

Of course, knowledge is more than just numbers and measures. In a free society, knowledge is also created and shared through verbal exchanges.[8] Societies that value freedom and prosperity protect their citizens' right to free speech, which greatly facilitates the discovery and dissemination of knowledge. In the realm of science, knowledge is created as researchers share, publish, discuss and challenge ideas and findings. Michael Polanyi characterized this process as the Republic of Science.

## REPUBLIC OF SCIENCE

Imagine if scientists worked in isolation, relying only on their own knowledge and ideas. Without access to the ideas and findings of other scientists, progress would be slow, with many missteps and much waste. When scientists are well-informed about the work of others and are free to choose which problems they will pursue, they learn and adjust their own efforts. Michael Polanyi described this "coordination by mutual adjustment of independent initiatives" as a "Republic of Science."[9]

Because initiatives are adjusted through self-coordination, a joint result is achieved that is "unpremeditated by any of those who bring it about." These kinds of initiatives cannot be directed centrally without undermining their effectiveness. The scientific community is innovative because it provides "a framework of discipline and at the same time [encourages] rebellion against it." It "enforces the teachings of science in general for the very purpose of fostering their subversion in [the] particular."

Polanyi argued that Adam Smith's and F. A. Hayek's model of a market system of mutual self-adjustment is simply a special case of his more general Republic of Science. A market economy provides this same combination of discipline and freedom. It requires the discipline of real value creation in order to profit while allowing freedom in how to create that value.

Just as entrepreneurs are not free from the discipline of the market, scientists are not free from the standards and norms of the scientific community. Knowledge advances as individual initiatives produce findings subject to the tests of evidence and criticism. This challenge process ensures any potential contribution to the body of scientific knowledge is validated before coming into general acceptance and use.

"The Republic of Science is a Society of Explorers" striving "towards an unknown future." "It is disciplined and motivated" by a mutual authority which is dynamic. It is "bent in its entirety" on constant self-renewal and continues its existence "by cultivating originality among its followers."

Seeking, sharing, discussing or challenging ideas and plans plays a crucial role inside an organization. None of us has all the knowledge to consistently make the best decisions or discoveries. Knowledge is dispersed and of various kinds; therefore, we need ways to ensure the relevant kinds are considered before making important decisions. When a workplace culture of respect and trust is promoted, employees share their ideas and seek out the best knowledge to anticipate and solve problems. Verbal exchanges lead to the discovery of new and better ways to create value. When such exchanges are hampered by overbearing taboos, procedures or hierarchy, knowledge sharing is stifled.

At KII, truth is what gets results consistent with Principle 1 of our MBM® Guiding Principles and stands the tests of evidence and criticism, not what someone in the hierarchy declares is true. Continual questioning and brainstorming to find a better way is what we call a challenge process.

The quality of this process depends on a willingness to respectfully engage in open, honest and objective debate, to challenge the status quo, and to consider humbly any challenges to our own beliefs, proposals and actions. This applies just as much to challengers as to those being challenged. Challengers need to participate with intellectual honesty in the spirit of constructive improvement, rather than opposing something because it was "not invented here."

## RICHARD WHATELY ON TRUTH

As the philosopher, economist and Anglican bishop Richard Whately observed: "It is one thing to wish to have truth on our side, and another thing to wish sincerely to be on the side of truth."[10]

Communication that fosters value creation requires constructive disagreement. An organization in which people work in isolated silos without a culture that promotes constructive challenges is one that will lose ground to competitors. If people only communicate good news, or if everyone pretends to agree, much less knowledge is generated and fewer discoveries are made. To be most effective, a challenge process must include people with different perspectives, kinds of knowledge and expertise.

One productive form of challenge process is a brainstorming session. It should include representatives of all the functions and capabilities that can contribute significant value to the discussion—business management, sales, operations, supply, technology, business development, public sector, etc. It may also be appropriate to include outsiders if they possess superior knowledge or a valuable perspective.

Another form of challenge process is the compliance audit. Some people may resist these because they feel threatened or worry that they aren't trusted. Instead, the audit should be viewed as a chance to learn and improve. Would you rather find out you have a problem this way or by having a disaster?

To drive the process of creative destruction internally, nothing can be immune to challenge. Each of us must help foster an open environment that invites challenge and embraces change. If you find that your views are rarely challenged, or that you rarely challenge the views of others, something is wrong. It may be the lack of entrepreneurial drive, the culture, or perhaps the incentives. Whatever the problem, it must be addressed lest it imperil the business. You should actively seek knowledge and alternative points of view. You must proactively share your knowledge and viewpoints with those who would benefit. When all participants in a challenge process embrace our MBM Guiding Principles and focus on creating value, the result is a powerful tool for discovery.

Decisions should be made using economic and critical thinking, logic and evidence, rather than emotion or gut feeling. We should be explicit about the mental models we are applying and communicate them clearly. Avoid unnecessary complexity by keeping things, as Einstein advised, "...as simple as possible but no simpler."[11] Elegantly articulated but complicated mental models, arguments and ideas that do not deliver profitable results have no value. Style should never take precedence over substance.

Market economies are exceptionally effective at communicating what people value and how best to satisfy those values. Within a company, market-based knowledge processes harness the powerful capability of markets to produce useful knowledge.

There are always better, faster and cheaper ways to create more value for a company and its customers. Value creation requires good economic thinking, measuring profitability whenever practical, seeking and sharing knowledge, embracing a challenge process and appropriately using proven tools and mental models. These are critical components of superior knowledge processes.

*"The market determines who shall [have what property and who shall do what work]. None of these decisions is made once and for all; they are revocable every day. The selective process never stops."*

Ludwig von Mises[1]

CHAPTER 6

# DECISION RIGHTS

*"In the market economy, every owner is continuously obliged to justify, through service, his right to retain control of the resources he claims. Otherwise, consumers peacefully transfer the ownership and control into more capable, more productive, more serviceable hands."*

—Paul L. Poirot[2]

*"Markets maximize benefits [when they are] supported by externally enforced property right rules that prohibit taking without giving in return."*

—Vernon Smith[3]

P rivate property is essential for both a market economy and prosperity. There cannot be a market economy without private property, and a society without private property cannot have prosperity. To ensure ongoing innovation in satisfying people's needs, there must be a robust and evolving system of private property rights.

Without a market system based on private property, no one can know how to effectively allocate resources. This is because they lack the information that comes from market prices. Those prices depend on voluntary exchanges by owners of private property. Prices and the resulting profit and loss guide entrepreneurs toward satisfying the needs of consumers. Through this system, consumers are able to direct entrepreneurs in efficiently allocating resources through knowledge and incentives in a way no central authority can.

# PROPERTY RIGHTS

Countries that clearly define and protect individual private property rights stimulate investment and grow. Those that threaten and confiscate private property lose capital and decline. They also lose the capability and efforts of the individuals who would be the greatest contributors to economic growth.

Problems also arise when property rights are unclear or ill-defined. In such cases, owners don't benefit from all the value they create and don't bear the full cost from whatever value they destroy. Their use of the property will not be optimally focused on creating value in society. In the past, when owners were not liable for injury to person or property caused by pollution, noise or accidents, they made less effort to prevent them. When rent controls have prevented landlords from charging market prices, buildings have been allowed to deteriorate.

The biggest problems in society have occurred in those areas thought to be best controlled in common: the atmosphere, bodies of water, air, streets, the body politic and human virtue. They all reflect aspects of the "tragedy of the commons" and function much better when methods are devised to give them characteristics of private property.

## THE TRAGEDY OF THE COMMONS

Garrett Hardin coined the phrase "tragedy of the commons" to describe herdsmen grazing animals on a commons (shared grazing lands).[4] He describes herdsmen asking themselves, "What is the benefit to me of adding one more animal to my herd?" Seeking his own gain as a rational herdsman, he will add as many as he can. He receives all of the proceeds when the additional animals are sold, but bears almost none of the cost of grazing these animals and depleting the commons. Hardin writes, "Each man is locked into a system that compels him to increase his herd without limit—in a world that is limited. Freedom in a commons brings ruin to all."

People tend to take better care of things they own. This is because the owners of a resource not only reap the benefits of its use, but bear the costs as well. When ownership is unclear, such that no one sufficiently benefits by preserving a resource (as when no one or everyone owns it), the resource tends to be overused, used inefficiently or even extinguished.

Oceans tend to be overfished due to lack of ownership. This example of the tragedy of the commons arises because fishermen only benefit when the fish are in their boat. There is little incentive for fishermen to leave fish in the ocean for someone else to catch. The size of their catch determines the benefit of their actions, while the cost—depleting stocks of fish—is shared by all fishermen.

Clear, dependable property rights that allow individuals to enjoy the benefits of ownership while bearing the full costs of their actions are the solution to the tragedy of the commons. This is just as true in a company as it is in society.

In a market economy it is consumers who ultimately direct the owner's use of property. They reward him if he serves them well and abandon him if he doesn't. Thus, if an owner satisfies consumers, his property rights increase. If he doesn't, they diminish. Property rights are constantly being earned by those who best use them to satisfy consumers.

We tend to think of private property in simple, concrete and constant terms such as fee ownership of land including mineral rights. But, as the market develops, private property rights become more specialized. They become subdivided and appear in new forms: leaseholds, partnership interests, stock securities, debt, mineral interests, intellectual property, contract rights, options and so on. This increased specialization in property rights creates additional value similar to increased specialization from a finer division of labor.

At Koch Industries, we use decision rights to attempt to replicate the beneficial roles of property rights in society. Decision rights can be thought of as property rights in the organization. We create decision rights by ensuring that employees have clearly defined roles, responsibilities, expectations and authorities.

Clear decision rights allow employees to allocate, consume or conserve the company's resources as they attempt to create value. They also enable employees to know what they are responsible for and to be held accountable, just like owners. Decision rights expand for those who consistently make sound, value-adding decisions and contract for those who do not.

Decision rights should reflect an employee's demonstrated comparative advantages. An employee has a comparative advantage among a group of employees when he or she can perform an activity more effectively at a lower opportunity cost than others. For example, selling is typically a comparative advantage of star sales people, even though they may also be very good at sales analysis. This gives sales analysts a comparative advantage at doing analysis, even when they are not as proficient at it as outstanding sales people. Employees who take account of their comparative advantages and consistently make good decisions will have expanding decision rights.

It is common to hear that the person with the best knowledge should make the decision. In general, this may be true, but it is more precise to say that it is best for the person with the comparative advantage to make the decision. Understanding the nuance between these two concepts leads to greater value creation.

None of us is equally gifted or equally weak in any one kind of intelligence or talent. All of us have the potential to make a unique contribution. Each person's contribution is based on his values, talent, knowledge, effort and experience compared with others. This uniqueness leads to the division of labor, a specialization of roles that improves the productivity of an organization.

## DIVISION OF LABOR

A fundamental factor leading to human well-being "is the division of labor and its counterpart human cooperation."[5] Specialization and exchange are much more effective at satisfying human needs than self-sufficient individuals working in isolation. The division of labor is responsible for the world's greatly increased standard of living in spite of the huge population growth.

The power of the division of labor flows from the diversity in humans and in nature. The benefits of specialization and exchange come from variations in skills, knowledge, culture, infrastructure, geography, natural resources, soil and climate. If every person and every part of the earth were equal in every way, there would be much less benefit from the division of labor.

Because no two people are alike in values, knowledge, skills or circumstance, it follows that even employees who have similar roles in an organization should have different kinds and degrees of decision rights. We should also expect decision rights to change over time, as our businesses and our comparative advantages change and we make good or bad decisions. This is a dynamic process meant to ensure that those with the best combination of values, knowledge, motivation, demonstrated capability and opportunity cost are making the decisions.

## ROLES, RESPONSIBILITIES AND EXPECTATIONS

We use RR&Es to define general areas of responsibility and accountability. Specific expectations accompany the responsibilities within a given role. A person is accountable if he or she will bear the consequences (good or bad) of a decision. Both the person making the decision and the person delegating are held accountable. This ensures that a culture of ownership, accountability and appropriate delegation is developed to avoid inaction, abdication or finger-pointing.

RR&Es require an ongoing dialogue involving the employee, supervisor and other interested parties. Each employee is responsible to ensure his or her RR&Es are current, accurate and effective. Both employees and supervisors are accountable for ensuring that RR&Es focus employees on maximizing their contribution to advancing the vision of their business or group. Supervisors must give employees honest and frequent feedback, and use performance reviews to help employees understand their performance relative to expectations and how to improve. Supervisors must not use a cookie-cutter approach to RR&Es, requiring those of each employee to be the same. This causes RR&Es to become meaningless and fails to help employees create value. Neither should RR&Es be confused with traditional job descriptions, which normally are generic summaries of tasks and duties. Instead, each employee's RR&Es should focus on value creation and be tailored to his or her individual comparative advantages and opportunities.

A role is not a job title. A role is a description of the position held and the functions performed by an individual. The number and types of roles in any organization will vary. They are determined by the nature of the business, the organization's vision, its strategies and the comparative advantages of the individuals responsible for executing those strategies.

Most of us have multiple roles in an organization at any given time. Each role has an associated bundle of responsibilities. These responsibilities clearly define the products, services, assets or processes for which we are accountable. The level and nature of that accountability is articulated in our expectations. Expectations are written statements specifying the results required of an employee if the business is to achieve its objectives. Expectations should always be clear, specific, and whenever possible, measurable. They should focus on the desired outcomes rather than on the activities that might be required to produce those outcomes. Expectations must also be open-ended and challenging enough to expand an employee's vision of what can be contributed to an activity. This encourages experimentation and innovation.

A clear understanding between an employee and supervisor (and anyone else affected) regarding priorities and expectations is critical. Expectations are most meaningful when they are measurable, even if the measures are subjective. There is a temptation for expectations to be closed-ended (for example, 67 carloads must be filled every day), rather than open-ended (maximizing the number of carloads filled to the extent that doing so is safe, compliant and profitable). The closed-ended form discourages innovation, while the open-ended form encourages the employee to think, engage and innovate. The open-ended form leads to ever-increasing value creation.

Decision rights and authorities constitute an employee's freedom to act independently in carrying out the responsibilities of a given role. They typically take the form of limits for different kinds of operating expenses, capital expenditures and contractual commitments. But they can also include discrete (that is, yes or no) authorities to make other decisions without supervisory approval, such as hiring or firing employees. The authority to make some decisions, but not others, is based on the degree to which an employee has demonstrated the ability to achieve results in different areas. For example, a Koch Supply & Trading leader who has demonstrated a superior ability to analyze trading strategies would have significant authority to approve trading positions. Only if he or she has also demonstrated the ability to select profitable traders, however, would that leader be granted the authority to hire or fire.

# PRINCIPLED ENTREPRENEURSHIP™

Those without the authority to make certain decisions are not exempt from entrepreneurial initiative. They can still create value. Sitting back and excusing yourself from action because you lack authority is unacceptable. Principled entrepreneurs in the marketplace face such challenges all the time. After identifying an opportunity, entrepreneurs must persuade investors, lenders, suppliers, customers and others to fund or otherwise support their vision for a new venture. Successful entrepreneurs are not deterred by their lack of authority to control resources.

As employees discover opportunities for innovations or improvements, they are expected to seek out others who have the authority to act on those ideas. We expect employees to use knowledge sharing, the challenge process, logic, evidence and the judicious use of our Decision Making Framework to earn approval for their ideas. Employee proposals, if approved and successfully executed, earn increased decision rights. Each employee must demonstrate the sense of urgency, discipline, accountability, judgment, initiative, economic and critical thinking skills, and risk-taking mentality necessary to generate the greatest contribution to the company. This is the essence of Principle 4, Principled Entrepreneurship.

Widespread value creation throughout a company requires: (1) that decision rights are not granted or bestowed, they are earned, and (2) lack of authority is not considered an excuse for inaction in the face of a problem that needs to be corrected or an opportunity that should be pursued. Instead, employees need to raise awareness, propose solutions and find a way to address the problem or capture the opportunity.

There is no excuse for failing to take a critical action, even in areas of shared responsibility. The problem of not having clear ownership can lead to the tragedy of the commons. It can be devastating, as when a government report is filled out improperly because the business leader, operations supervisor and compliance specialist all assume someone else is responsible.

Proximity to a problem or process does not determine who is in the best position to make a decision. In a world characterized by knowledge-driven rapid change, top-down decision-making is commonly criticized as being highly inefficient. It is true that centralized command-and-control business management suffers from many of the same problems seen in centrally planned economies.[6] Those with local knowledge are often in a better position to solve the problem at hand. The ideas and creative energy of all employees should be leveraged, but universally decentralized decision-making has its own problems. Some decisions, if made at the local level, can be unprofitable because a broader perspective is required.

The mindless application of either approach—universally centralized or completely decentralized decision rights—is not the answer. For example, decisions about how to gain optimum throughput from a refinery at any given time probably are best made by people on site. On the other hand, people further removed, but with broader knowledge, may be better positioned to make a decision on what the most profitable product mix will be in five years. Decisions should be made by those with the best knowledge, taking comparative advantage into account.

Individual authorities will vary widely. So will individual performance, which is driven by differing values, experience, capability and opportunity. Authorities tend to be lower with new, unproven employees, whether they are newly hired or veterans of an acquired company. Years of experience, credentials or titles have not proven to be reliable predictors of good decision-making ability. Only demonstrated success in decision-making reveals an individual's decision-making ability, and then, only for that type of decision.

When done well, the process of defining and continually updating every individual's RR&Es and corresponding authorities creates enormous benefits for the business and the employee. This process establishes clear priorities, individual ownership and accountability for results, as well as scorecards for compensation. It fosters awareness and the discovery of changing comparative advantages among the many members of an organization. It is also an essential step in connecting individual employees to the vision and strategies of their particular businesses. It focuses them on the activities that will most profitably achieve that business unit's goals. Most important, it continually improves the ability to make sound, value-adding decisions as a company.

In a market economy, the combination of well-defined and protected property rights, the right culture, useful knowledge and incentives from prices and profit and loss spontaneously lead to a network of relationships that maximizes value and creates prosperity and progress. In a company, the combination of a well-designed decision rights process, good values, knowledge sharing, measures and incentives brings about a spontaneous order that maximizes value creation and growth.

*"The problem of management"* is *"how to set up social conditions in any organization so that the goals of the individual merge with the goals of the organization." This "includes the needs for meaningful work, for responsibility, for creativeness, for being fair and just, for doing what is worthwhile and for preferring to do it well."*

Abraham Maslow[1]

# CHAPTER 7

# INCENTIVES

*"To the economically illiterate, if some company makes a million dollars in profit, this means that their products cost a million dollars more than they would have without profits. It never occurs to such people that these products might cost several million dollars more ... without the incentives to be efficient created by the prospect of profits."*

—Thomas Sowell[2]

*"The only combination of rewards and feedback that seems to improve motivation is rewards that depend not only on doing the task, but upon how well it is done plus informational feedback."*

—Charles Murray[3]

**P**rofit is a powerful incentive that inspires entrepreneurs to be alert and take risks to anticipate and satisfy customer demands. Finding less expensive ways to make existing products and developing new and better ones is not only profitable for the discovering entrepreneur, it is beneficial for society.

The quality of people's lives is improved when more highly valued products and services become available with the consumption of fewer resources, leaving more to satisfy other needs in society.

At Koch, we use incentives to attempt to align the interests of each employee with the interests of both the company and society. This means we strive to pay employees a portion of the value they create for the company. We believe this approach tends to attract and retain the right people, and motivates them to be principled entrepreneurs.

History offers numerous powerful examples of the influence of incentives in determining the nature of outcomes. The importance of proper incentives was one of the earliest lessons learned in the colonization of America. When the Pilgrims came to America in 1620, all their property, including their houses and crops, was held in common. Everyone worked for the collective, with equal rewards to all no matter how much a person contributed. This system led to deprivation and even starvation. It "was found to breed much confusion and discontent and retard much employment," Governor William Bradford recounted later.[4] The most capable men and women did not want to receive the same compensation as those who were lazy or inefficient. Often colonists simply didn't go out to the fields to work because they felt the system was unfair.

After two-and-a-half terrible years, Bradford decided to give each family its own plot of land, to reap from it whatever they could. That was the beginning of Plymouth Colony's prosperity. Because they were able to keep what they earned, the Pilgrims had the incentive to work hard and create wealth.[5]

Another example, taken from Charles Bateson's *The Convict Ships*, demonstrates the power of incentives to change even the behavior of unscrupulous people.[6] During the 18th century, when ship captains took on the responsibility of taking criminals from England to Australia, they were paid for every criminal loaded onto their ships in London. This encouraged a captain to pack as many criminals onto the ship as possible, regardless of the health and safety of the prisoners, for a six-month journey. To make matters worse, many captains hoarded the food meant for the prisoners and sold it upon arrival. Those lucky enough to reach Australia were "lean and emaciated" and "full of filth and lice."

Ships sailing under this reward system experienced high mortality rates with one ship losing nearly one-third of its prisoners. This led "to modification of [the] payment with the object of preventing an excessive mortality." Instead of paying only for each prisoner that got on the boat, the program was changed so that a portion was withheld and paid for each prisoner that got off the boat alive and well in Australia. The "financial incentive to treat convicts humanely" dramatically improved the conditions and survival rate of the prisoners. The first three ships sailing under the new approach experienced only two deaths out of 322 prisoners. This system kept mortality rates low and ensured "the gross abuses earlier practiced were almost entirely eliminated."

Putting aside the question of the original captains' lack of character, it is a simple truth that people respond to incentives. Some believe that individuals should not need to be rewarded to do the right thing, that people should be motivated by duty, compassion or loyalty rather than self-interest. Unfortunately, even people with good character and intentions aren't always able to resist perverse incentives. Although the Pilgrims had the courage to brave hazardous seas and a forbidding land, they only behaved in a way that allowed them to survive and prosper after the proper incentives had been put in place.

More recently, we have witnessed the transformation of entire countries, such as Ireland, following a beneficial change in incentives and related factors. In 1988, *The Economist* concluded that Ireland was "an economic failure" and "heading for catastrophe."[7] The Deputy Prime Minister of Ireland, Mary Harney, admitted that the government had been on a "borrowing, spending and taxing spree that nearly drove us under. It was because we nearly went under that we got the courage to change."[8] Among other things, corporate tax rates were reduced from 50 percent to 12.5 percent, much lower than today's European average of 30 percent.[9]

The results exceeded even the most optimistic expectations. Ireland's economy grew by 83 percent during the 1990s compared to 18 percent in the 1980s and the European average of 22 percent in the 1990s. Ireland's unemployment rate fell from 18 percent in the late 1980s to less than 5 percent in 2005. GDP per capita grew from US$12,000 in 1990 to US$36,000 in 2002, making it the second-most prosperous country in Europe. In 1997, *The Economist* revised its earlier prediction, declaring Ireland to be "Europe's shining light."[10]

While this chapter focuses on incentives for employees, incentives are also important in aligning the interests of a company's other constituents, such as customers, suppliers, shareholders, distributors, agents, communities and governments. By properly aligning the incentives of all our constituents, we greatly improve our ability to succeed. An understanding of subjective value is essential for creating these incentives.

For example, rather than paying outside sales agents a low percentage of total sales, we pay a much higher percentage of the sales price above our opportunity cost. This gives the agent a strong incentive to achieve a price that maximizes our risk-adjusted profit instead of sacrificing price to improve the chances of making the sale. We also strive to make it more profitable for a retailer to preferentially promote our products. By understanding their unique operation, we can determine how to motivate them to provide us premium shelf space and get their sales people to recommend our products. Likewise, we believe communities and governments are more likely to allow companies to grow and prosper when those firms are leaders in environmental, safety and other regulatory compliance. Everyone benefits when new and better jobs are created by practicing Principled Entrepreneurship™.

The Pilgrims, convict ships and Ireland examples are not meant to demonstrate that everyone needs incentives to do the right thing every time, but that proper incentives result in both good and bad people doing the right thing more often. Proper incentives motivate people to work harder, be more creative, and create more value for others and, hence, themselves.

These are not, however, the only reasons for using incentives. Even when well-intentioned and motivated people are eager to succeed, they still face the challenge of understanding where and how to focus their time and effort. Successful entrepreneurs use the incentives of the market to determine the most productive course of action. Likewise, employers should use incentives to guide employees toward areas where their attention and effort can create the most value.

Structuring incentives to bring about productive behavior without adverse unintended consequences is challenging. Proper incentives must not only motivate employees to create value and signal what is valued, they must also motivate employees to create that value in a principled manner. To design effective incentives, we must first have an understanding of human action.

## HUMAN ACTION

Ludwig von Mises posits that three requirements must be present for individuals to take action.[11] These are: (1) unease or dissatisfaction with the present state of affairs, (2) a vision of a better state, and (3) belief that they can reach the better state.

We mow our lawns only when we are dissatisfied with their present condition, believe they will look better and know how to mow them. Customers switch when they become dissatisfied with their current supplier, believe another supplier will serve them better and are able to switch. When just one of these requirements is missing, people will not act.

Companies that fail to provide conditions that meet all three requirements create a culture of inaction. Companies that encourage creative destruction, provide a vision of how to create value and facilitate decision making, create a culture of Principled Entrepreneurship.

What any individual employee values is highly subjective and includes both financial and non-financial components. Possible non-financial incentives include belief in what we are doing, challenge, competition, pride, recognition, satisfaction, enjoyment, helping others succeed and being part of a successful team. Our Beaverhead Ranch in Montana provides an example of incentives that are a mixture of financial and non-financial. Recognizing that people don't go into ranching for the money but for the lifestyle, of which a big part is working with their families, the policy of not allowing family members to work on the ranch was changed. Further, houses were built on the ranch for each family. The ranch immediately attracted a far superior work force.

In MBM®, the ideal incentive for each employee is what best motivates that employee to maximize value for the company over his or her career. Where feasible, compensation should be tailored to each individual employee's subjective value, providing the highest value to the employee for a given cost to the company. Incentives should take into account the individual's risk profile, time preference and the most-valued form, amount and variability of compensation. For example, employees with a low time preference might discount deferred compensation less than their company, which would tend to do so at its cost of capital. Consequently, deferring compensation might have a lower cost to these employees than to their company. In such a case, other factors being equal, compensation should be more heavily weighted toward a longer term.

## TIME PREFERENCE

Other things being equal, people prefer the satisfaction of a given value now, rather than later. This time preference varies from person to person and for the same person at different periods. Compared to an individual with a lower time preference, individuals with a high time preference are more likely to seek satisfaction today rather than save.

The degree of your time preference is the amount of additional satisfaction required in the future for you to give up a unit of satisfaction now. The ratio of these differing valuations represents the price of time, not money, and is the reason for interest. This originary interest is distorted by inflation and complicated by credit risk.

When property rights are clearly defined and respected, time preference decreases, individuals are more willing to save and businesses are more willing to invest long term.

To understand what is important to specific employees, managers must establish open and honest relationships with them. The difficulty in accomplishing this will vary with the role, the manager, the employee and the manager's experience with the employee. Each manager and each employee is unique.

For some employees, non-financial incentives such as being praised for a job well done can be as important as financial incentives. But care must be taken to ensure that such praise is truly earned. As Maslow put it: "To be praised for what one does not deserve or to have one's accomplishment unduly exaggerated can actually be guilt-producing."[12] False praise also tends to undermine trust.

The principle that should guide the implementation of all financial incentives is that they encourage the innovation and creative destruction necessary to maximize long-term sustainable profitability. Even though optimum compensation can never be determined with precision, the value an employee has contributed should be determined as accurately as possible. A judgment can then be made as to the optimum form and amount of compensation.

## PERVERSE INCENTIVES

Most employees want to make a positive contribution and do the best they can for themselves, the company and society. Unfortunately, many companies have incentives such that employees benefit by undermining long-term value for the company. Only an exceptional person can resist perverse incentives for long.

Some companies institute fixed budgets as a way of controlling costs. Under this system, profitable opportunities are often missed as managers reject profitable proposals that would cause their budgets to be exceeded. It is also common for a company to attempt to reduce costs by ordering an across-the-board 10 percent reduction in budgets or people. This practice usually results in removing profitable expenditures and people along with unprofitable ones, tending to make the company less rather than more profitable. Both approaches create perverse incentives. Perverse incentives are common in company/employee (principal/agent) relationships, and are known as an agency problem.

An agency problem tends to be created whenever a principal, or owner, hires an agent, or employee. It is the principal's wish that the agent's actions are in the best interest of the principal, while the agent typically wants what is best for the agent.

These conflicting interests manifest themselves in various ways. In cases where the principal and the agent have different risk profiles, the problem typically takes one of two forms. In the first, employees are extremely risk-averse, generally due to leadership failing to reward profitable risk-taking, while excessively penalizing losses from prudent risk-taking. The result is a play-it-safe culture.

To discourage this behavior, value creation should be rewarded and losses penalized only when appropriate. Prudent risk-taking should be encouraged by applying the concept of opportunity cost. Within limits, the profits forgone from a missed opportunity should be considered the same as losses from a failed venture. The value of missed opportunities, as well as other shortcomings, should be estimated, included in evaluations of the employee's performance and communicated to the employee. This eliminates the incentive to forgo riskier opportunities that are in the company's interest, such as an employee who chooses an investment with a 90 percent chance of making $100,000 over one with a 50 percent chance of making $1 million. Consideration of opportunity cost also helps eliminate waste in the approval process, including excess steps and analysis that jeopardize opportunities by making it impossible to get approvals quickly and efficiently.

In the other extreme, employees take imprudent or even unauthorized risks. In these cases, individuals hope to make a great deal of money for themselves by going for broke, even if it puts the company at risk. Such rogue employees, operating out of personal interest at the expense of the general interest, have destroyed entire companies, as happened to the venerable Barings Bank in 1995. This behavior is minimized by selecting and retaining employees, foremost, on values and beliefs, appropriately setting and enforcing decision rights and having effective controls.

Another type of perverse incentive faced by publicly traded companies is even more prevalent. Management at these companies is under a great deal of pressure to meet quarterly earnings forecasts. Falling slightly short can cause a significant drop in the stock price. Consequently, management is motivated to make decisions that optimize short-term earnings at the expense of maximizing real long-term value. Such decisions may include under-investing in attractive cyclical or long-term opportunities, ignoring problems that, if recognized, would force writedowns, or even manipulating the books. Perverse incentives make managing a public company long term extremely difficult. They also make it easy to understand why Koch Industries prizes its private status.[13]

# ALIGNING INCENTIVES

A successful system of incentives must align the individual interests of employees with the general interests of the company. If a result will be good for the employee, it must also be good for the company, and vice versa. If the result will be bad for the company, it must also be bad for the employee. This is especially true in all areas of compliance. To conduct business otherwise invites disaster. The effectiveness of our compliance program increased dramatically once we began holding everyone involved accountable, especially those in the management chain.

The first goal, then, is to provide incentives that harmonize the interests of the individual with those of the company. This reinforces the individual's natural desire to do the right thing to help the company prosper. Second, compensation should be consistent with the notion that no two employees are alike, and thus their contributions can vary considerably. Third, no limit should be put on an employee's compensation so employees will not put a limit on the value they create. Finally, incentives should be structured in a way that effectively attracts, motivates and retains principled entrepreneurs.

These goals are accomplished by rewarding achievement that contributes to the long-term value of a company. By refusing to reward activities that do not produce results, a process is created that beneficially guides behavior and motivates individuals to do the right thing. As a result of differences in vision, desire, values and ability, people do not always take advantage of the nearly limitless opportunities to create value. This is why two employees performing similar roles will quite likely be compensated differently. This mirrors the entrepreneurial incentives of a free market economy.

Think about value creation broadly. Employees create value not only by innovating or capturing an opportunity, but also by helping keep the whole value creation process (the business) running smoothly. For example, financial functions are essential in providing information to guide business decisions. Providing useful information in a timely and cost-effective manner can be as important to long-term profitability as developing new products and should be recognized and appropriately rewarded.

Confusing as it might seem, failure and getting results are not mutually exclusive. When driving experimental discovery within a company, failures should be expected. It is important to recognize that today's positive results may be derived from lessons learned from yesterday's failed experiments.

To be clear, our organization does not reward failure. Although we expect it on occasion, we strive to avoid it. In addition to learning from our failures, we must recognize whether the failure resulted from poorly thought-out or impulsive action, or belongs to that percentage of failures to be expected from prudent risk-taking, such as well-designed experiments or bets.

Encouraging experimental discovery and not penalizing well-planned experiments that fail fuels an engine of small and frequent bets that generates powerful discovery and learning. This is vital to innovation, growth and long-term profitability. Companies should avoid a sense of entitlement regarding compensation. Automatic raises (such as cost-of-living adjustments[14]) and pay formulas based on titles, certificates, diplomas, seniority or experience—such as the Hay system—are destructive compensation schemes. So are bonuses paid for performance relative to budgets, rather than for value created.

As should now be clear, our approach is different from typical pay systems. Many of these evaluate positions rather than individuals and are designed to establish rigid pay structures across similar positions within a company. They combine such factors as the number of direct reports, training and education credentials, job complexity and authority levels into a formula that produces a suggested compensation range for a given position. This tends to discourage real value creation through innovation, discovery and entrepreneurial behavior. Instead, it fosters empire building and bureaucratic or political behavior.

At Koch Industries, we do not reward roles. Rather, we reward people for specific contributions and results, not for some generalized or averaged result. Karl Marx famously summarized Communism as a system that takes "from each according to his ability" and redistributes "to each according to his needs." MBM says, in contrast, "From each according to his ability, to each according to his contribution."

## MARGINAL CONTRIBUTION

Being able to estimate an employee's marginal contribution is an important element in an effective compensation system. Marginal contribution is a specific application of marginal analysis. It refers to the portion of value created that can be assigned to a specific change, factor or individual. Understanding an employee's marginal contribution requires answering several questions: What results were achieved? Would the opportunity have been captured without the employee? What would the results have been without this individual? How did this employee contribute to our culture? At Koch companies, we also evaluate how well the employee lives by our MBM Guiding Principles.

An employee's performance should be tracked throughout the year, not just at year-end. Economic analysis and 360-degree feedback should be used to understand his or her contribution to long-term results. This is to ensure the best information available is used to appropriately recognize both positive and negative contributions. The evaluation should include any carryovers from uncompensated contributions in previous periods. Positive and negative carryovers often result from projects put in motion long ago. Either the projects were not completed by the end of the measurement period or the results had not yet been achieved. Koch companies do not reward projected results we only hope to realize. Instead, we reward results as we develop evidence they are being realized.

Salary, properly seen, is an advance payment for the future value an employee is expected to create for the company. So what happens when an employee adds more value than was originally reflected in his or her salary? The employee shares in that extra value, just like an entrepreneur in the marketplace.

There are several tools for accomplishing this, including annual incentive compensation, spot bonuses, multi-year rolling profit-based compensation and other incentives. A key role of managers is to retain and motivate employees who are adding superior value by paying for value created and ensuring competitiveness. Even when an employee is profitable, further improvement in performance is always possible. A supervisor should communicate how both the company and the employee would benefit from this improvement. Employees who embrace and internalize this feedback will increase their contribution.

Conversely, unprofitable employees, those who create less value than their compensation and other costs, are wasting the organization's resources and destroying value. Such cases need to be dealt with quickly.

Abraham Maslow said: "All human beings...prefer meaningful work to meaningless work."[15] To do meaningful work is to contribute—to create value in society. In a true market economy, a measure of the value created in society is profit. Getting incentive systems right does more than align our interests and signal what is valued. Appropriately recognizing achievement encourages employees to lead productive lives, realize their full potential and find satisfaction and fulfillment in their work.

"*To achieve the greatest fulfillment, we must passionately learn, challenge and experiment to create value as we apply sound theory and practice in every aspect of our lives.*"

Charles G. Koch

CHAPTER 8

# LESSONS LEARNED

*"Doctors of [the 15th century] kept their secrets locked in languages their patients could not read. To attack this citadel demanded a willingness to defy the canons of respectability, to uproot oneself from the university community and from the guild. Such a venture required as much passion as knowledge, and more daring than prudence. To open the way, a man needed the knowledge of a professional and yet not be committed to the profession. He should be in the physician's world but not of it."*

—Daniel Boorstin[1]

*"Innovation is the specific tool of entrepreneurs, the means by which they exploit change as an opportunity for a different business or a different service. It is capable of being learned, capable of being practiced. Entrepreneurs need to search purposefully for the sources of innovation, the changes and their symptoms that indicate opportunities for successful innovation. And they need to know and to apply the principles of successful innovation."*

—Peter Drucker[2]

M BM® is the application of the Science of Human Action in an organization. It is a proven process for taking the principles that lead to prosperity in society and applying them in an organization in a way that gets results. I believe MBM is applicable to all types of organizations—not only businesses but also charitable, governmental, social and other groups. However, this book is focused on how we apply it in Koch companies. Fundamental to consistently creating value with MBM is understanding the ways it can be misapplied.

## PITFALLS

One form of misapplication is the failure to recognize that MBM is a holistic system. Its real power is in the underlying philosophy and its integrated application, not in the form or the parts. Those who have gained only a conceptual or procedural understanding, but not personal knowledge, tend to misapply it.

For this reason, before an organization can successfully apply MBM, its leaders must gain personal knowledge through a dedicated commitment to understanding and holistically applying MBM to achieve results. Gaining this personal knowledge involves self-modification that starts with understanding the underlying concepts. It also requires seeing how the concepts contribute to long-term profitability, and then repeatedly applying them over time.

This is a difficult undertaking. Given human nature, leaders and practitioners frequently fail to act consistently with their stated philosophies. This problem has existed throughout history for organizations of all types—governments, religions, non-profits, as well as businesses. Such a shortcoming results in cynicism, form over substance, bureaucracy, command-and-control, or destructive, self-serving behavior. People attempting to apply MBM are not exempt from this failing.

Another misapplication involves trying to apply MBM via prescribed, detailed steps, rather than by teaching and reinforcing its philosophy and providing useful tools (models). Instead of developing RR&Es or improvement initiatives using the joint knowledge of supervisors and employees, we have, at times, mistakenly dictated their content. Compliance programs have sometimes been implemented through bureaucratic procedures, rather than by setting the standards and expectations that enable people to innovate. Misapplications such as these put us in the same trap as the government's wasteful approach to regulation, mandating the exact methods to be used, rather than setting and enforcing science-based standards. We have even, on occasion, treated relatively harmless deviations from an internal procedure the same as violations of a government mandate.

Our project analysis process, the Decision Making Framework, is intended to be applied in a manner that is as simple as possible but no simpler. Unfortunately, the DMF has, at times, been made so burdensome and complicated that it has discouraged good projects. Analysis that doesn't improve a decision tends to be waste. This becomes evident when the same analysis is done for a simple $2 million project as a complex $100 million one. One method of eliminating this waste is for leaders to ask preparers what work they did that wasn't valuable to them in preparing the analysis. Similarly, preparers need to be told what portion of their analysis wasn't useful to those making the decision. Whatever work was not valuable to either should be eliminated for similar projects.

On the other hand, unprofitable or even worthless investments have resulted when the DMF hasn't been used at all, has been used by those who didn't really understand it or has been misused to justify ill-conceived pet projects. Everyone's time is wasted when the preparer doesn't truly understand and misapplies the DMF. In all DMFs, the key bets need to be identified and analyzed and the underlying assumptions verified.

But the extent of the analysis and verification should vary tremendously according to the risk/reward, size, complexity and regulatory requirements of the project. This process should be guided by what will maximize risk-adjusted profits. A highly profitable, low-risk project may require almost no steps at all, that is, immediate approval. When MBM is applied bureaucratically as a rigid formula, it is not really MBM. Fundamental to MBM is the principle of spontaneous order, in which we provide general rules to enable people to innovate by challenging the status quo. Remember, MBM teaches that enforcing detailed procedures causes the general rules that encourage value creation to break down.

Other misapplications include turning MBM into a set of meaningless buzzwords, or worse, using it to justify what someone already does or wants to do. Employees have used the local knowledge model to rationalize their desire to do whatever they want without supervisory challenge. Another distortion was "charts for Charles," where employees wastefully went through the motion of applying the form of MBM without any attempt to get value from it.

To avoid these pitfalls, to truly make MBM work, we must have leaders with the necessary understanding and insight who develop the ability and mechanisms to spot and correct these misapplications early on. As customers and competitors change, entrepreneurs in a market economy are continually put in a position of having to adjust to optimally create value. Fortunately, entrepreneurs have a powerful feedback mechanism that enables them to make those adjustments: profit and loss. We need to develop the mechanisms that enable us to quickly make similar adjustments in the way we apply MBM. Despite misinterpretations and misapplications, MBM has proven to be extremely powerful when interpreted and implemented appropriately. It has enabled us to grow tremendously over the last 40-some years. The power of MBM has been released when employees have applied its spirit, not its form, by internalizing the MBM mental models through repeated application. It has worked when employees have used the best knowledge in making decisions and innovations, when we have used it as a philosophy and set of tools to help us create value, and when we have continually asked ourselves, "Is this creating value?" All interpretations and applications should be tested with this question.

# INNOVATION

We have learned the hard way that creating value with MBM requires that we develop the personal knowledge and the feedback mechanisms to build a culture of Principled Entrepreneurship™. Such a culture engages everyone in a passionate pursuit of innovation toward an unknown future of ever-greater value creation.

Innovation, not just in technology but in all aspects of business, is the key to long-term success. When a business improves faster than its competitors and potential competitors, it grows. When it falls behind, it becomes the victim of creative destruction. Discoveries require a change in vision so that the facts and relationships we think we understand can be viewed from a different perspective. This can be stimulated by being outward-rather than inward-looking, as when time is spent understanding customers. Changing our vision requires humility and can be painful. Innovation begins with a passionate preoccupation with a problem and the courage to pursue a solution. It demands personal commitment and a great deal of focused intellectual and emotional energy.

The process of discovery requires personal knowledge and begins with a mindset that constantly seeks out gaps between what is and what could be. Our searching leads us to hypotheses, or hunches, which, although they can't be fully articulated, drive us toward an explanation. The next step is the clear articulation of our hypotheses, which enables us to put the discovery in a usable form.

So how is this discovery process facilitated? Polanyi believed that discoveries best occur in a system of spontaneous order, of mutually adjusting individual initiatives. He likened this process to a group trying to solve a giant jigsaw puzzle. The rate of discovery is highest when everyone works together in sight of each other, so that every time a piece fits, the others are alerted to opportunities for the next step. The rate of discovery is lower when the solution is centrally directed or when each person works the puzzle separately.

## POLANYI ON PUZZLE SOLVING

"Imagine that we are given the pieces of a very large jig-saw puzzle, and suppose that for some reason it is important that our giant puzzle be put together in the shortest possible time. We would naturally try to speed this up by engaging a number of helpers; the question is in what manner these could be best employed. The only way the assistants can effectively co-operate, and surpass by far what any single one of them could do, is to let them work on putting the puzzle together in sight of the others so that every time a piece of it is fitted in by one helper, all the others will immediately watch out for the next step that becomes possible in consequence. Under this system, each helper will act on his own initiative, by responding to the latest achievements of the others, and the completion of their joint task will be greatly accelerated. We have here in a nutshell the way in which a series of independent initiatives are organized to a joint achievement by mutually adjusting themselves at every successive stage to the situation created by all the others who are acting likewise."[3]

To begin creating such a system of discovery based on spontaneous order, employees' roles must include making and encouraging innovations. This requires an environment in which people don't blindly follow marching orders; rather, ideas are encouraged and challenged but not destructively criticized. The challenge process must be seen as an opportunity to learn and improve, not as a chance to kill another person's idea or as a sign of failure. To be most creative, people should work as teams sharing ideas, not in isolated silos, and they must be provided sufficient resources and time. People must also make time by forgoing less-important work.

Innovation is facilitated by having the right people in the right roles with the right skills and values. It is enhanced by seeking critical feedback from others who have a diversity of knowledge and perspectives. It also requires a culture in which exploration, experimentation and discovery are not stifled by fear of failure. And the culture must be reinforced by incentives that reward the prudent risk-taking necessary for innovation.

Discovery necessitates a framework of discipline while simultaneously encouraging a rebellion against the status quo. The need for plausibility and commercial value requires enforcing the appropriate methodology, while the need for originality requires encouraging dissent. In short, innovation entails the right combination of discipline and freedom.

Since the future is unknown and unknowable, those contributing to innovation must be given every possible encouragement and a latitude consistent with their performance and capabilities. At the most fundamental level, MBM is a philosophy and methodology to encourage innovations that create value for both a company and society. If this book facilitates such value creation, it will have served its purpose.

# APPENDIX A

## PRODUCTS TRADED

### PETROLEUM
Crude oil
Condensate

### REFINED PRODUCTS
Gasoline
Jet fuel
Fuel oil
Diesel fuel
Resid

### PETROCHEMICALS
Paraxylene
Orthoxylene
Metaxylene
Cumene
Pseudocumene
Toluene
Benzene
Propylene
Ethylene
Waste fiber and polymer

### FINANCIAL
Fixed income (credit)
Equity arbitrage
Real estate
Tax exempt leases
Municipal bonds
Corporate bonds
Equities
Asset-backed securities
Credit default swaps

Foreign exchange
Interest rates

### MINERALS
Exploration and production properties
Petroleum coke
Coal
Sulfur
Cement
Slag
Shipping

### ENERGY
Natural gas
Electrical power
Emission credits

### NATURAL GAS LIQUIDS
Ethane
Propane
Butane
Natural gasoline

### STRUCTURED PRODUCTS
Risk management
Derivatives

### METALS
Aluminum
Aluminum alloy
Copper
Lead
Zinc
Tin

Nickel
Steel
Silver

### FERTILIZER
Anhydrous ammonia
Urea
UAN

### FOREST PRODUCTS
Pulp and paper
Recycled fiber
Wastepaper
Timber
Woodchips
Plywood

### AGRICULTURE
Soybeans
Wheat
Corn
Cotton
Sugar
Cattle
Hogs
Cocoa
Canola
Orange juice
Milk

### INTERMEDIATE FEEDSTOCKS
Naphtha
Gas oil
Ethanol

# APPENDIX B

## MAJOR BUSINESS GROUPS

**FLINT HILLS RESOURCES**
Petroleum refining, chemicals, lube stocks and asphalt.

**KOCH MINERAL SERVICES**
Minerals trading and distribution, and exploration and production.

**KOCH PIPELINE**
Crude oil and refined products pipelines.

**KOCH SUPPLY & TRADING**
Trades numerous commodities.

**KOCH NITROGEN**
Nitrogen fertilizer manufacture, distribution and trading.

**KOCH QUANTITATIVE TRADING**
Trades proprietary financial instruments.

**KOCH CHEMICAL TECHNOLOGY GROUP**
Mass transfer equipment, burners and flares, heat exchangers, membrane separation systems and engineering services.

**KOCH FINANCIAL**
Municipal and other finance, financial guaranty reinsurance, collateralized debt obligations and credit default swaps.

**INVISTA**
Nylon fiber, polymer and intermediates, spandex fiber, polyester polymers and resins, specialty chemicals and PTA licensing.

**GEORGIA-PACIFIC**
Consumer products, packaging, containerboard, bleach board, fluff and market pulp, structured panels, wood products, gypsum and chemicals.

# APPENDIX C

## BUSINESSES EXITED

Crude oil gathering
Gas processing
Sulfuric acid
Tankers
Drilling rigs
Dredge manufacturing
Specialty chemicals
Sulfur plant design
Cryogenic systems
Air quality consulting
Grain trading
Meat processing
Microelectronic
  chemicals
Pizza dough

Animal feed
Grain milling
Coal mining
Fiberglass products
Medical equipment
Tennis court surfaces
Ammonia pipelines
Broadband trading
Service stations
Propane retailing
Activated carbon
Cooling towers
Business aircraft
Trucking
Canadian pipelines

Commercial lending
Telecommunications
Image transmission
Gas pipelines
Platinum trading
Carbon dioxide
Chromatography
Slag cement
Power generation
Feedlots
Performance roads
Gas liquids
  gathering
Particle board

# PARTIAL LIST OF MBM® MODELS

ABC process
Apprentice
As simple as possible,
    but no simpler
Challenge process
Change
Comparative advantage
Competitive advantage
Competitive analysis
Compliance
Conflict resolution
Continuous improvement
Core capabilities
CPV triangle
Creative destruction
Customer focus
Decision Making Framework
Decision rights
Dispersed and tacit knowledge
Diversity, specialization
    and the division of labor
Economic freedom and
    prosperity
Economic vs. political means
Experimental discovery
Externalities and public goods
Fatal conceit
Feedback
Financial statements and
    economic reality
Form vs. substance
Franchise development

Freedom of speech and
    standards
Fulfillment
Hierarchy of needs
Human action
Humility and intellectual
    honesty
Incentives
Innovation
Integration of theory and
    practice
Integrity
Internal markets
Knowledge processes
Law of scientific proof
Marginal analysis
Marginal utility
Mental models
Mobility of labor
Multiple intelligences
Operations excellence
Opportunity cost
Origination
Ownership and accountability
Personal knowledge
Political economy
Praxeology
Price seekers vs. price takers
Price-setting mechanism
Principled Entrepreneurship™
Prioritization
Private property

Profitability measures
Public sector
Republic of Science
Requirements for action
Respect
Risk, uncertainty and options
Role of prices and profit and
    loss
Roles, responsibilities and
    expectations
Rule of law
Rules of just conduct
Science of Liberty
Self-interest
Spontaneous order
Structure of production
Subjective value
Sunk cost

Theory of constraints
Time preference
Trade
Trading
Tragedy of the commons
Transaction costs
Transactional excellence
Value chain analysis
Value creation
Values required for prosperity
    and progress
Virtue and talents
Vindictive triumph
Vision
Vision Development Process
Waste elimination
Whole vs. the parts

# NOTES

## CHAPTER 1 Evolution of a Business

1. Fred C. Koch, "Random Advice on a Business Career." Speech given at the University of Wichita, Wichita, Kan., April 1960.
2. H. G. Bohn, *A Handbook of Proverbs*, 1855.
3. T. Levitt, "Marketing Myopia" *Harvard Business Review*, 1960, July–August.

## CHAPTER 2 The Science of Human Action

1. F. A. Hayek, *Individualism and Economic Order*. University of Chicago Press, Chicago, Ill., 1980, p. 101.
2. Cited by W. A. M. Alwis, "Spoon-Feeding in 'Do' Disciplines," *CDTL Brief*, Vol. 3, No. 2, p. 5.
3. Fred C. Koch, "Random Advice on a Business Career." Speech given at the University of Wichita, Wichita, Kan., April 1960.
4. Joseph Schumpeter, *Capitalism, Socialism and Democracy*. Harper, New York, 1950, p. 83.
5. Ludwig von Mises, *Human Action*. Regency Co., Chicago, Ill., 1963, p. 32.
6. Michael Polanyi, *Personal Knowledge*. University of Chicago Press, Chicago, Ill., 1974, p. 60.
7. Cited by Robert Sobel, "Past and Imperfect: History According to the Movies," *Electronic News*, Vol. 42, Issue 2124, p. 52.
8. Thomas Hobbes, *Leviathan*. Adamant Media Corp., Boston, Mass., 2005, p. 84.
9. W. Edwards Deming, Video Series, 1988–1990.

10. Michael Polanyi, *Personal Knowledge.* University of Chicago Press, Chicago, Ill., 1974, p. 151.

11. Franz Oppenheimer, *The State.* Fox and Wilkes, San Francisco, 1997, pp. 14–15.

## CHAPTER 3   Vision

1. Michael Polanyi, *Personal Knowledge.* University of Chicago Press, Chicago, Ill., 1974, p. 144.

2. James Allen, *As a Man Thinketh.* Andres McMeel Publishing, Kansas City, Mo., 1999, p. 58.

3. The real economic contribution of an enterprise is its long-term profitability above opportunity cost, that is, above its cost of capital.

4. Adam Smith, *An Inquiry into the Nature and Causes of the Wealth of Nations.* Liberty Fund Inc., Indianapolis, Ind., 1981, pp. 26–27.

5. Alexis de Tocqueville, *Democracy in America.* Harper and Row Publishers, New York, 1969, p. 526.

6. Vernon Smith, "Constructivist and Ecological Rationality in Economics," Nobel Prize lecture, Stockholm, Sweden, December 8, 2002.

7. Richard Epstein, "Coercion vs. Consent," *Reason,* Vol. 35, No. 10, pp. 40–50.

8. Adam Smith, *An Inquiry into the Nature and Causes of the Wealth of Nations.* Liberty Fund Inc., Indianapolis, Ind., 1981, p. 456.

9. F. A. Hayek, *The Fatal Conceit.* University of Chicago Press, Chicago, Ill., 1989, p. 77.

10. George Will, "How Houston Slipped on the Oil Patch," *Washington Post,* January 17, 1988.

11. F. A. Hayek, *Individualism and Economic Order*. University of Chicago Press, Chicago, Ill., 1980, p. 101.

12. Cited by Scott Thorpe, *How to Think Like Einstein: Simple Ways to Break the Rules and Discover Your Hidden Genius*. Sourcebooks, Naperville, Ill., 2000, p. 149.

## CHAPTER 4    Virture and Talents

1. 1812 letter to John Adams.

2. Rhetoric i. c., 322 BC.

3. Frederic Bastiat, *Selected Essays on Political Economy*. The Foundation For Economic Education, Inc., New York, 1964, p. 56.

4. Howard Gardner, *Frames of Mind: The Theory of Multiple Intelligences*. Basic Books, New York, 1983, pp. 3–70 and *Changing Minds*. Harvard Business School Publishing, Boston, Mass., 2006, pp. 27–42.

5. As described by Karen Horney in *Neurosis and Human Growth* (pp. 17–39), those who degenerate into self-idealization can become extremely destructive. Normal drives "toward self-realization are shifted to the aim of actualizing the idealized self" or "the search for glory." The most destructive stage "is the drive toward a vindictive triumph" in which the goal is to hurt others as revenge for real or imagined humiliations. Each vindictive triumph adds to feelings of grandeur and the compulsion to destroy anyone who challenges this warped self-image. The elation does not last, so the quest for revenge is renewed and carried out with utter disregard for truth and the person's own best interests.

6. Selection is a continuous process that applies to all of us all the time. Although we tend to think of it only with regard to hiring new employees, it applies to existing employees as well. This is simply another expression of creative destruction.

7. Kenneth Arrow, *The Limits of Organization*, Norton, New York, 1974, p. 23.

## CHAPTER 5 Knowledge Processes

1. Thomas Sowell, *Knowledge and Decisions*. Basic Books, New York, 1980, p. 215.

2. Cited by Carol Krucoff, "The 6 O'Clock Scholar," *Washington Post*, January 29, 1984.

3. Samuel T. Coleridge, *Aids to Reflection and the Confessions of an Inquiring Spirit*. George Bell and Sons, London, 1893, p. 36.

4. Failure to do so is generally referred to as "the knowledge problem," which the market process solves. See F.A. Hayek, *Individualism and Economic Order*. University of Chicago Press, Chicago, Ill., 1980, pp. 77–91.

5. Cited by Scott Thorpe, *How to Think Like Einstein: Simple Ways to Break the Rules and Discover Your Hidden Genius*. Sourcebooks, Naperville, Ill., 2000, p. 3.

6. John Wooden and Steve Jamison, *Wooden: A Lifetime of Observations and Reflections on and off the Court*. Contemporary Books, Chicago, Ill., 1997, p. 94.

7. Some aspects of GAAP require financial statements to be presented in a way that we believe doesn't reflect economic reality or doesn't best reveal profit drivers, problems or opportunities. In these cases we prepare our internal statements in the way that provides the most useful information and then modify them to comply with GAAP for external publication. An example which demonstrates this point is the requirement that fixed manufacturing costs be inventoried and released through cost of sales when the product is sold. An approach providing more useful information is to expense period costs as incurred. At one Koch business, the GAAP approach caused an over-

statement of profits due to inventory buildup during a period
of significant new capacity additions. This caused a delay in
our response to the deterioration in market structure.

8. By verbal exchanges, we mean both oral and written. Examples
include newspapers, magazines, scientific and trade publica-
tions, broadcast news, books, conferences, phone calls, e-mails,
Web logs (blogs), conversations with customers and suppliers,
rating agency reports, telephone directories, vendor advertising,
and so on.

9. Michael Polanyi, *Knowing and Being*. University of Chicago
Press, Chicago, Ill., 1969, pp. 50, 51, 54, 55 and 70.

10. Richard Whately, *Essays on Some of the Difficulties in the
Writings of St. Paul, and in Other Parts of the New Testament*.
B. Fellowes, London, 1830, p. 33.

11. Cited by Scott Thorpe, *How to Think Like Einstein: Simple
Ways to Break the Rules and Discover Your Hidden Genius*.
Sourcebooks, Naperville, Ill., 2000, p. 35.

## CHAPTER 6  Decision Rights

1. Ludwig von Mises, *Human Action*. Regency Co., Chicago, Ill.,
1963, p. 308.

2. Paul Poirot, "Ownership as a Social Function," *Toward Liberty*,
Vol. 2, Institute for Humane Studies, Menlo Park, Calif.,
1971, p. 296.

3. Vernon Smith, "Some Economics and Politics of Globali-
zation," Speech given at North Carolina State University,
Raleigh, N.C., March 2, 2005.

4. Garrett Hardin, "The Tragedy of the Commons," *Science* 162,
1968, pp. 1243–1248.

5. Ludwig von Mises, *Human Action*. Regency Co., Chicago, Ill.,
1963, p. 157.

6. Mises called the challenge faced by government central planners the "economic calculation problem," which formed the basis of his argument that true socialism was an unworkable system. A centrally planned economy lacks the market signals—prices and profit and loss—that enable entrepreneurs to optimally allocate scarce resources to meet the highest-value needs of consumers.

Central planners have no such mechanisms to solve the knowledge and articulation problems they face. They cannot know people's subjective values or how subjective values, technology, tastes and diminishing returns are changing. Nor can they respond to these changes in real time. As Sowell indicated (see p. 95), they also cannot provide the necessary articulation of the characteristics of the products to be produced, such as the quality and relative quantity of different-sized nails.

## CHAPTER 7 Incentives

1. Abraham Maslow, *Toward a Psychology of Being*. John Wiley and Sons, Hoboken, 1988, pp. 244–245.

2. Thomas Sowell, "Profits without Honor," www.townhall.com, December 23, 2003.

3. Charles Murray, *In Pursuit of Happiness*. Simon and Schuster, New York, 1988, p. 152.

4. William Bradford, *Of Plymouth Plantation: 1620–1647*. Modern Library, New York, 1967, p. 133.

5. Stephen Innes, *Creating the Commonwealth and the Economic Culture of Puritan New England*. W. W. Norton and Co., New York, 1995, p. 62.

6. Charles Bateson, *The Convict Ships: 1787–1868*. Brown, Son and Ferguson, Glasgow, 1969, pp. 20–21.

7. *The Economist,* "Poorest of the Rich," January 16, 1988, p. 55.

8. Thomas L. Friedman, "The End of the Rainbow," *New York Times,* June 29, 2005.

9. Marc A. Miles, Kim R. Holmes, Mary A. O'Grady, Ana I. Eiras, Brett D. Schaefer and Anthony B. Kim, *2006 Index of Economic Freedom.* Heritage Foundation, Washington D.C., 2006.

10. *The Economist,* "Ireland Shines," May 17, 1997, p. 16.

11. Ludwig von Mises, *Human Action.* Regency Co., Chicago, Ill.,1963, pp. 13–14.

12. Abraham Maslow, *Eupsychian Management.* R.D. Irwin, Homewood, Ill., 1965, p. 28.

13. Arguments have been made that shareholders of public companies are best served by maximizing share price in the short term. However, when this results in sacrificing long-term profitability, there is a flaw in the way equity markets work. Our philosophy is clear: Profit by creating real, long-term value by the economic means while faithfully following our MBM Guiding Principles.

14. Managers need to have a thorough understanding of what the market is paying for any given role they supervise and where each individual fits in that market range with respect to his or her marginal contribution. While we focus on determining an employee's contribution when considering compensation, we also recognize the need to comply with any legal or contractual obligation, such as those in union contracts.

15. Abraham Maslow, *Eupsychian Management.* R.D. Irwin, Homewood, Ill., 1965, p. 26.

## CHAPTER 8 Lessons Learned

1. Daniel Boorstin, *The Discoverers.* Random House, New York, 1983, pp. 338–339.

2. Peter Drucker, *Innovation and Entrepreneurship.* HarperCollins, New York, 1993, p. 1.

3. Michael Polanyi, *Knowing and Being.* University of Chicago Press, Chicago, Ill., 1974, pp. 50–51.

# BIBLIOGRAPHY

Allen, J. (1999) *As a Man Thinketh*. Kansas City, Mo.: Andres McMeel Publishing.

Alwis, W. A. M. (2000) "Spoon-Feeding in 'Do' Disciplines," *CDTL Brief,* Vol. 3 Number 2.

Armentano, D. T. (1982) *Antitrust and Monopoly: Anatomy of a Policy Failure*. New York: Wiley.

Arrow, Kenneth (1974) *The Limits of Organization*. New York: Norton.

Ashton, T. S. (1948) *The Industrial Revolution: 1760–1830*. New York: Oxford University Press.

Bastiat, F. (1964) *Selected Essays on Political Economy*. New York: The Foundation For Economic Education.

Bateson, C. (1969) *The Convict Ships: 1787–1868*. Glasgow: Brown, Son and Ferguson.

Bohn, H. G. (1855) *A Handbook of Proverbs*.

Boorstin, D. (1983) *The Discoverers*. New York: Random House.

Bradford, W. (1967) *Of Plymouth Plantation:* 1620–1647. New York: Modern Library.

Coleridge, S. T. (1893) *Aids to Reflection* and *The Confessions of an Inquiring Spirit*. London: George Bell and Sons.

Davies, B. (1992) *The Thought of Thomas Aquinas*. New York: Oxford University Press.

Deming, W. E. (1988–1990) "The Complete Deming Management Library," video series.

Drucker, P. (1993) *Innovation and Entrepreneurship*. New York: HarperCollins.

Durant, W. (1935) *The History of Civilization*. New York: Garden City Publishing.

___, (1953) *Story of Philosophy: The Lives and Opinions of the World's Greatest Philosophers*. New York: First Pocket.

*The Economist* (1988) "Poorest of the Rich," Jan. 16, p. 55.

___, (1997) "Ireland Shines," May 17, p. 16.

Epstein, R. A. (2004) "Coercion vs. Consent," *Reason*, Vol. 35 Issue 10, pp. 40–50.

Friedman, T. L. (2005) "The End of the Rainbow," *New York Times*, June 29.

Gardner, H. (1983) *Frames of Mind: The Theory of Multiple Intelligences*. New York: Basic Books.

___, (2006) *Changing Minds*. Boston, Mass.: Harvard Business School Publishing.

Hardin, G. (1968) "The Tragedy of the Commons," *Science* 162, pp. 1243–1248.

Harper, F. A. (1957) *Why Wages Rise*. New York: The Foundation for Economic Education.

Hayek, F. A. (1979) *The Counter-Revolution of Science*. Indianapolis, Ind.: Liberty Press.

___, (1980) *Individualism and Economic Order*. Chicago, Ill.: University of Chicago Press.

___, (1982) *Law, Legislation and Liberty*. London: Routledge.

___, (1989) *The Fatal Conceit*. Chicago, Ill.: University of Chicago Press.

___, (1994) *The Road to Serfdom*. Chicago, Ill.: University of Chicago Press.

Higgs, R. (1987) *Crisis and Leviathan*. New York: Oxford University Press.

Hobbes, T. (2005) *Leviathan*. Boston, Mass.: Adamant Media Corp.

Horney, K. (1991) *Neurosis and Human Growth*. New York: Norton.

Innes, S. (1995) *Creating the Commonwealth: The Economic Culture of Puritan New England*. New York: W. W. Norton.

Jefferson, T. (2004) *Quotations of Thomas Jefferson*. Bedford, Mass.: Applewood Books.

Johnson, P. (1985) *Modern Times*. New York: Harper and Row.

Koch, F. C. (1960) "Random Advice on a Business Career," University of Wichita address, April.

Kolko, G. (1963) *The Triumph of Conservatism*. New York: Free Press.

Krucoff, C. (1984) "The 6 O'Clock Scholar," *Washington Post*, Jan. 29.

Kuhn, T. S. (1962) *The Structure of Scientific Revolutions.* Chicago, Ill.: University of Chicago Press.

Lavoie, D. (1985) *National Economic Planning: What Is Left?* Cambridge, Mass.: Ballinger Publishing.

Levitt, T. (1960) "Marketing Myopia," *Harvard Business Review,* Reprint R0407L.

Locke, J. (1978) *Second Treatise on Civil Government.* Grand Rapids, Mich.: W. B. Eerdmans Publishing.

Mackay, C. (1995) *Extraordinary Popular Delusions and the Madness of Crowds.* New York: Crown Trade Paperbacks.

Maslow, A. H. (1954) *Motivation and Personality.* New York: Harper.

___, (1965) *Eupsychian Management* (republished as *Maslow on Management).* Homewood, Ill.: R.D. Irwin.

___, (1988) *Toward a Psychology of Being.* Hoboken: John Wiley and Sons.

Miles, M. A., K. R. Holmes, M. A. O'Grady, A. I. Eiras, B. D. Schaefer and A. B. Kim (2006) *The 2006 Index of Economic Freedom.* Washington, D.C.: Heritage Foundation and Dow Jones & Company, Inc.

Mises, L. v. (1963) *Human Action.* Chicago, Ill.: Regency Co.

___, (1969) *Bureaucracy.* New York: Arlington House.

Murray, C. (1994) *Losing Ground.* New York: Basic Books.

___, (1988) *In Pursuit of Happiness.* New York: Simon and Schuster.

Oppenheimer, F. (1975) *The State.* San Francisco, Calif.: Fox and Wilkes.

Poirot, P. (1971) "Ownership as a Social Function," *Toward Liberty* Vol. 2, Menlo Park, Calif.: Institute for Humane Studies, Inc.

Polanyi, M. (1969) *Knowing and Being.* Chicago, Ill.: University of Chicago Press.

___, (1974) *Personal Knowledge.* Chicago, Ill.: University of Chicago Press.

Porter, M. (1983) *Competitive Strategy.* New York: Free Press.

___, (1985) *Competitive Advantage.* New York: Free Press.

Rosenberg, N. and L. E. Birdzell (1986) *How the West Grew Rich.* New York: Basic Books.

Schumpeter, J. (1950) *Capitalism, Socialism and Democracy.* New York: Harper.

___, (1989) *Business Cycles.* Philadelphia, Pa.: Porcupine Press.

Simon, J. (1995) *The State of Humanity.* Cambridge, Mass.: Blackwell and the Cato Institute.

Smith, A. (1981) *An Inquiry into the Nature and Causes of the Wealth of Nations.* Indianapolis, Ind.: Liberty Fund, Inc.

Smith, V. (2002) "Constructivist and Ecological Rationality in Economics," Nobel Prize lecture, December.

___, (2005) North Carolina State University address, March.

Sobel, R. (1996) "Past Imperfect: History According to the Movies," *Electronic News,* Vol. 42 Issue 2124.

Sowell, T. (1980) *Knowledge and Decisions.* New York: Basic Books.

___, (1981) *Ethnic America.* New York: Basic Books.

___, (1987) *A Conflict of Visions.* New York: Quill.

___, (2003) "Profits without Honor," www.townhall.com, Dec. 23.

Thorpe, S. (2000) *How to Think Like Einstein: Simple Ways to Break the Rules and Discover Your Hidden Genius.* Naperville, Ill.: Sourcebook.

Tocqueville, A. (1969) *Democracy in America.* New York: Harper and Row Publishers.

Weaver, P. H. (1942) *The Suicidal Corporation.* New York: Simon and Schuster.

Whately, R. (1830) *Essays on Some of the Difficulties in the Writings of St. Paul, and in Other Parts of the New Testament.* London: B. Fellowes.

Will, G. (1988) "How Houston Slipped on the Oil Patch," *Washington Post,* Jan. 17.

Wooden, J. and S. Jamison (1997) *Wooden: A Lifetime of Observations and Reflections on and off the Court.* Chicago, Ill.: Contemporary Book.

Wriston, W. B. (1997) *The Twilight of Sovereignty.* Bridgewater, N.J.: Replica Books.

# INDEX